The Heresy of Wu Han

His play 'Hai Jui's Dismissal' and its role in China's Cultural Revolution

At the centre of China's Cultural Revolution in its first stages stands the ambiguous figure of Wu Han. Deputy mayor of Peking and protege of the eighth-ranking figure in the Chinese Communist Party hierarchy, Wu Han occupied until the mid-sixties a favoured position among the intellectual elite of the People's Republic, and was already well known and respected as an essayist when in 1959 he began publishing a series of essays and a play on the virtuous Ming Dynasty official Hai Jui. His Peking Opera *Hai Jui's Dismissal,* following in 1961, was performed all over China. Gradually, to the intelligentsia at whom these works were primarily aimed, it became apparent that Wu Han was using Hai Jui to lampoon Chairman Mao Tse-tung and the core policies of the Chinese Communist Party. The name Hai Jui began to have a double meaning for many who had become disenchanted with Mao's rule. Other dissidents began to pen articles and plays on similar themes.

For several years after 1959, when he appears to have temporarily lost control of the Central Committee of the Party, Mao chafed under these literary attacks. He bided his time and grouped his forces, and in late 1965 he sprang. From an obscure newspaper editor named Yao Wen-yuan came a sudden, scathing attack on Wu Han and his play. This attack marks the beginning of the Cultural Revolution. Before it was over, China's intellectuals would suffer a crushing setback, the entire Peking Municipal Party Committee would be dismissed, the ranks of the Party's leadership would be decimated, Yao Wen-yuan would become one of the most powerful men in China, and Mao Tse-tung would regain his supremacy in the Party.

A few western observers are aware that Wu Han's play sparked the convulsion, but none have seemed sure of its contents. This publication marks the first translation of this key document in the Cultural Revolution into any western language. In addition, the analytical and historical part of Mr Ansley's work, by charting the Chinese reaction to the play and examining the charges made against Wu Han, helps to clarify the obscure origins of a cataclysmic national phenomenon that was at once intellectual, social, and political.

It is thus a work of scholarly as well as documentary literary value, and while it will be essential to specialists in current Asian affairs, it will also be of wide interest to all those interested in contemporary Chinese writing and politics.

CLIVE ANSLEY studied at the University of British Columbia, concentrating on Chinese history and the relationship between nationalism and communism in Vietnam and Indonesia. In 1966, at the height of the Cultural Revolution, he toured China visiting Canton, Peking, Chengchow, Loyang, and Shanghai. He is now teaching in the Department of Asian Studies at the University of Windsor.

The heresy of **wu han**

His play 'Hai Jui's Dismissal' and its role in

China's Cultural Revolution

Clive Ansley   University of Toronto Press

© University of Toronto Press 1971
  Reprinted in paperback 2017
  University of Toronto Press, Toronto and Buffalo
  ISBN 978-0-8020-1665-2 (cloth)
  ISBN 978-1-4875-9813-6 (paper)

Contents

Acknowledgments

It is with great pleasure that I acknowledge at the outset the substantial aid rendered me by Professor Li Chi of the Department of Asian Studies, University of British Columbia. She spent countless hours of her time with me and I am sure there were moments when the rate of my progress caused her to feel the project would never be completed. It was only through Professor Li's assistance that some of the more obscure classical allusions occurring in the dialogue of this play were deciphered.

I am also indebted to Mr Raymond Lo, who gave me considerable linguistic assistance in my examinations of many of the documents I had assembled on the Great Cultural Revolution in China. In addition, I would like to express my thanks to Mrs Melody Kilian, Miss Dale Evans, and my mother, Mrs Emily Ansley, all of whom typed portions of the original manuscript, and to Mrs Patricia Kingsbury who typed the final version in its entirety. Part of the manuscript was read by Mr Neil Burton, who made a number of helpful suggestions and corrections. Several suggested revisions by Professors E.G. Pulleyblank, W.L. Holland and René Goldman, have been incorporated in the work as it now stands.

Although I express my gratitude to all those mentioned above, none of them is in any way responsible for the book in its final form. I alone take full responsibility for any errors of fact or presentation.

About the author of
Hai Jui's Dismissal

Wu Han was born in 1909 in the province of Chekiang. Although he came from a poor family, he supported himself through university and eventually became one of modern China's most prominent historians and a leader in the Chinese intellectual community. He is also known for his extensive knowledge of literature. Among Wu's published works are *Mirror of History, The Biography of Chu Yuan-chang, Javelin-throwing,* "On Hai Jui," and "Hai Jui Sends a Memorial to the Throne." He is also the editor-in-chief of the *Pocket Edition of Geographical Books.*

From 1930 to 1934, Wu Han attended Tsinghua University on a half-work, half-study basis. From 1934 to 1937 he lectured in Ming history at Tsinghua. Then, in 1937, he became a professor of history at Yun-nan University and the Southwest Associated University at Kunming. After the Second World War he was again a professor at Tsinghua (1946-48), and while there he did underground work for the Chinese Communists. He was Dean of the College of Arts and Head of the Department of History at Tsinghua from March of 1949 to February of 1950.

Wu had joined the China Democratic League (CDL) in 1944, and he never did become a member of the Chinese Communist Party. Nevertheless, he has held a very great number of political and cultural posts in Communist China. He was a standing member of the First National People's Political Consultative Committee from September 1949 to December 1954. During the same period he served on the board of directors of the Sino-Soviet Friendship Committee. From November 1949 to October 1951 he served as deputy mayor of Peking. In October 1951 the administrative structure of Peking was reorganized and Wu Han became deputy mayor in the new Peking Municipal People's Government. He continued in this post until his political demise in 1966. From 1949 to 1956 he was a standing member of the First Central Committee of the CDL. In August 1954 he was elected a deputy for Peking to the First National People's Congress. He was re-elected for a second term in August 1958, and for a third term in September 1964.

From June 1955 Wu was a member of the department of philosophy and social sciences in the Chinese Academy of Sciences. In February of 1956 he led a cultural delegation to India on behalf of the Sino-

Indian Friendship Association, and in April of the same year was elected to the board of directors of this body. In 1958 he led a song and dance troupe on a visit to France. He has also played leading roles in the China Afro-Asian Society and the Sino-Nepalese Friendship Association. In February of 1958 Wu became a member of the Scientific Planning Commission of the State Council, to undertake planning for the republication of classical works. He became president of the Peking Television University in 1964 and vice-chairman of the Chinese People's Committee for World Peace in 1965. The above functions constitute only some of the most notable aspects of Wu Han's career. Since 1949 he has in addition served in many other capacities far too numerous to be listed here.

In November 1965 *Hai Jui's Dismissal,* and Wu Han personally, came under scathing attack in a Shanghai newspaper article. It was the publication of this article which launched the Great Cultural Revolution. Eventually Wu and several people close to him were specifically charged with having colluded with China's enemies within and without. Subsequently they disappeared from public view. The details of these events are described and analysed in part II.

1 'Hai Jui's Dismissal' by Wu Han
Translated by Clive Ansley

Preface

I do not have an understanding of plays, nor do I see them very often. This is especially true of Peking Opera. Although I lived for many years in Peking when I was studying at the university, I didn't see it even once. These last few years there have been comparatively many opportunities to see plays, but for this reason or that, I could never take advantage of them. Because of this, one could say that so far as Peking Opera is concerned I am a genuine dilettante. There are people who joke about my cultural level and I heartily agree with them. Isn't it really something to be wondered at, not only that a man like me has written a play, but that the play he has written is a Peking Opera?

You say this is strange. Certainly it is strange. Actually, when all is said and done, it is not so strange.

Things happened in this way. In 1959 I was doing research on Hai Jui and I wrote several essays concerning him. It was sometime around the end of that year that the Peking Opera dramatist, Ma Lien-liang, and a few other friends sought me out. They wanted me to discuss Hai Jui and after we had finished talking they asked me to prepare an outline, saying they wanted to produce a play. I was delighted to accept the responsibility, but after I thought about it very carefully I saw that the situation was not so wonderful. First, what to write? Second, how to write it? The first time I attempted this totally unprecedented undertaking, I felt very uncertain. I thought about it for a long time and tried to start writing several times, but none of my efforts seemed very much like an outline. I thought to myself that my effort was so pitiful that I would have to throw in the towel. I hesitated for a long time but I felt embarrassed to renege, so there was no choice but to summon all my courage and do what I had promised to do. With the outline uncompleted, I would just try to write a play. When I had written out a draft, I would ask my dramatist friends to revise it. By doing things in this manner I could make it a little more convenient for them. And so I set to work on it.

Unexpectedly, once I got into the saddle, I was unable to dismount. After the dramatic group and other friends had read the first draft, they said they thought it was all right as a draft. I had originally felt that now it was in their hands and that revising it was not my affair. But after having discussed it, my dramatist friends urged me to rewrite it and expressed quite a few opinions concerning it. In just this way – writing a draft, debating it, rewriting it – from beginning to end, I

3

rewrote it seven times, and that is still not taking minor changes into consideration. I had one mimeographed volume and two printed ones distributed among those of my friends who knew something about plays, and asked for their advice. We had a few dress rehearsals with the drama group, and a few specialists expressed a great many viewpoints. The great majority of them I accepted and used as a basis for revision. After the play was staged publicly, it was published in *Peking Literature and Art*.[1] Now, on the basis of the opinions of a few friends, I have made some changes in certain parts. By actual calculation, a year's time was required from the first germination to the seventh and final draft, every rewriting taking two or three days. From the first performance to the present time is almost another year. Quite a lot of time has been expended, and the writing really required much energy. Although I was considerably disheartened while in the midst of it, and thought of washing my hands of it, since things had already come as far as they had, I determined to do it and just went on doggedly.

Before trying to start writing, I decided on two fundamental principles. First, I was not going to write about Hai Jui's entire life, but only about one chapter in the story of his life struggle, because if I was to write a biography of Hai Jui the required time would be so long, the themes and characters so many, that it would be easy to commit the error of being insipid and to develop the defect of undue verbosity. It would not be easy for such a play to achieve prominence. Second, I did not want to rewrite plays already in existence. Quite aside from old plays, there are new ones, like *Hai Jui Sends a Memorial to the Throne,* by comrade Chou Hsin-fang of Shanghai. Although I haven't seen it, I know it has already been staged and so how could I write about the same episode again? It is necessary that one policy cover the whole nation. But for the entire nation to have the same subject matter in its plays is, in my opinion, absolutely unnecessary. Having considered it over and over again, I decided to write about the period, slightly more than half a year, from the summer of 1569 to the spring of 1570, particularly the events surrounding the appointment of Hai Jui to the office of Ying T'ien governor and the circumstances of his elimination of the tyrant landlords and the return of the land. The play was originally called simply *Hai Jui.* Afterwards quite a few friends pointed out that what was written in this play represented only a fraction of Hai Jui's life, and only then did I change the name to *Hai Jui's Dismissal.*

The changes which occurred in the course of the seven rewrites were in general concerned with the following problems.

The first is the central theme. The central theme of the first four drafts was designed to emphasize the orders Hai Jui gave the oppressive gentry to return the property which they had usurped from the common people, thus provoking the united opposition of the gentry so that he was dismissed from office and had to return home. The elimination of the bad gentry was just used as an embellishment for the story, as a sidelight to the returning of the land. A number of friends pointed out that while Hai Jui's ordering the return of the land was unquestionably factual historically, under the conditions of the time it was impossible for him not to solve the problems of the peasants at the same time. Measuring them by the standards of historical development, these kinds of political measures are definitely reformist. What would be the meaning of new historical dramas written today and propagating the reformism of history? I considered this problem many times and finally made the elimination of the bad gentry the central theme, relegating the returning of the land to the sidelines. This was a major change.

The second thing concerned the details of the story. The drama uses the misfortunes of a single family, that of the peasant woman Hung A-lan, to explain clearly the class contradictions of this era and the internal contradictions of the ruling class. After the second draft had been printed and distributed, a number of friends said that it was history but not drama, that it lacked complexity, that the climax was not very exciting, and that the contradictions were not presented sharply enough. The words they used were very polite but what they were really saying was that it was simply not a play. Because I am basically not a playwright or literary expert, my friends did not demand too much. In the fourth draft I added the scene "Meeting Hsü," allowing Hai Jui to first go and make a call on Hsü Chieh. Hsü Chieh stands with the gentry and wants Hai Jui to deal severely with wicked people and be strictly just in upholding the law, until Hai Jui asks about the case of Hung A-lan. But then Hsü Chieh immediately refutes the charges. Moreover, he says that if there is any proof of the crime, he will resign himself to the law and let it take its course. Then, in the scene "Asking a Favour," Hai Jui uses Hsü Chieh's words against him, presses him closely, and allows him no escape. I painstakingly carved out the dispositions and styles of work of the two opposing characters in these two scenes. My friends read it and thought that there was a little drama in it, but still not enough.

As for the case of Hung A-lan, I originally wrote it so that Hai Jui came in ordinary clothes to take up his post and overheard the peasant masses discussing the case in front of the Official Welcoming Pavilion.[2] While still in the middle of writing it, I revised it so that after Hai Jui had met with Hsü, he paid an incognito visit to Heng Yun Mountain[3] and received the real facts of the case. My friends all thought that if I was going to handle it this way, it would be necessary to add another scene. Finally, I wiped it all out and went back to the original method.

In the course of my several rewritings, I had already added the two scenes, "Discussing the Reception" and "The Feast of the Lanterns," in order to introduce Hai Jui's past through the mouths of other people and to express the praise of the local people for his benevolent rule. "Discussing the Reception" portrays the great tension of the officials of Soochow and Sungkiang prefectures on the evening before Hai Jui takes office. Everyone meets at the house of Huang Chin, the eunuch who is superintendent of the Imperial Silk Factory, in order to hear about the situation from him. There really was such a man as Huang Chin. After Hai Jui had sent in the memorial to the throne, the Chia Ching Emperor[4] was in a rage. He wanted to send some men to guard Hai Jui so as not to allow him to escape. At this time, Huang Chin was at the side of the Chia Ching Emperor. He said that there was no need for this action for he had heard that Hai Jui had already taken leave of his family and friends and had put his last affairs in order; that this man was very strong and resolute and absolutely incapable of running away. As soon as the Chia Ching Emperor heard these words he was dumbfounded. This scene, "Discussing the Reception," just makes use of Huang Chin for foreshadowing. At the beginning of the scene, because Hai Jui is coming, Huang Chin orders the subordinate eunuchs to decrease the number of sedan chair attendants by half. After the government officials have arrived, they hear from Huang Chin the details of Hai Jui's experience in memorializing the throne and being imprisoned. By the time of the scene "Feast of the Lantern Festival," he has already received the news that Hai Jui had been dismissed from office. When he goes out to see the lanterns, the subordinate eunuchs have already prepared the four-man sedan chair. Once more he says that this is unsatisfactory and that he now wants one with eight bearers. The subordinate eunuchs ask why and Huang Chin says that Hai Jui is leaving. What follows is just the common people celebrating the Feast of the Lantern Festival and lighting lanterns in the atmosphere of Ao Mountain.[5] Singing and dancing are employed. From the mouth of each person come songs dealing with the time since Hai Jui took up his post and with the changes which this half year has brought in their lives.

There was yet another revised draft of this "Feast of the Lanterns" scene. It had Hai Jui coming back from superintending the labourers on the Wusung River, preparing wine and meats, and passing the festival together with his mother and wife. The changed situation of this half year is brought out through the discussions of the members of the family. Before they are finished eating, a messenger sends in the *Peking*

Gazette.[6] By imperial decree, Hai Jui is transferred from his original position to that of superintendent of the Nanking Granary. Subsequently, another messenger arrives with a *Peking Gazette* stating that there is no need to establish a special position for the Nanking Granary. It is to be reunited with the Board of Revenue and Population. They do not dismiss him from his new post; they just pull the rug from underneath him by cancelling the post. Having Hai Jui read the differing contents of these two papers serves the function of making his thoughts known to the audience. I studied these two dramatic scenes many times but for the sake of diminishing the number of characters and themes, I ended by throwing it all out.

The third thing is the change in the ending of the story. In the original few drafts the final scene was "The Sendoff," in which Hai Jui is depicted leaving his post in ordinary clothes with the common people all accompanying him to the Official Reception Pavilion. From the mouths of the common people come songs telling of their longing, affection, and friendship for Hai Jui. In the midst of all this is inserted an episode in which the new governor, Tai Feng-hsiang, assumes office and is welcomed by Hsü Chieh and a group of officials. Hai Jui meets him personally, and knowing he is the newly-appointed governor, just wants to ask him not to change the new administrative practices which have developed in the last half year. But Tai Feng-hsiang attacks Hai Jui, saying that it is precisely because of these practices and because he has terrorized and fleeced the people and oppressed the gentry that the Emperor has dismissed him from office. Hsü Chieh also jeers him from the sidelines. Flushed with indignation, Hai Jui contradicts him. The two factions of the feudal ruling class, left and right, close in a face-to-face struggle. Finally, in the face of angry voices of the people, Tai Feng-hsiang and Hsü Chieh run for their lives like rats, frightened out of their wits. Hai Jui and all the others exit together. This scene of the play underwent many rewritings and dress rehearsals but everyone was dissatisfied with it. They felt that Hai Jui left in a dull and dismal manner, that all the emotional effect of the play was dissipated, and that it was wishy-washy. This was no way to handle the ending. My dramatist friends pointed out that if I rewrote this scene of the play with Hai Jui handing down a sentence of decapitation in the court, it would be somewhat stronger. However, according to historical fact, Hsü Chieh's son was only exiled for ten years and was certainly not put to death. Would it be reasonable to handle things in this way? Only after changing it several times did I finally make the decision to have Hsü Ying put to death. What I then rewrote became the present *Hai Jui's Dismissal.* When Hai Jui was in the throes of his verbal struggle with Tai Feng-hsiang, he as usual cared nothing that everyone was against him. Having sentenced Hsü Ying to be executed, he would hand over his seal of office and leave his post only after the sentence had been carried out. When it was written this way, quite a few of my friends thought it comparatively improved. But there was still another opinion. Some felt that if there were to be still another change, that if after the sentencing the emperor were to send someone with a special pardon, it would still be impossible to kill Hsü Ying and this would add still another twist to the plot. As for this opinion, up to the present time I have been unable to decide. It would be a good thing not to kill him but that still does not solve the problem of the dullness of the mood. In the end, how should it be correctly handled? The only thing to do was to wait for a while and listen to still more opinions before forming another plan.

In the process of making many revisions, not only was the content very greatly changed, but so was the literary form. In the rhyming of the first few drafts, I followed the *Shih Yün*[7] strictly. Afterwards some of my friends told me that it was not necessary to have it like this and that I could take a few more liberties. They said that the rhyming of Peking Opera had its own conventions. Secondly, the sung verses were basically of four, eight, or twelve lines, but sometimes they were also of three or five. My friends said that this was not satisfactory and that verses of three or five lines could be used only in exceptional circumstances. In addition, the poem at the end of a scene was sometimes four lines and sometimes two. My friends said it was best to have two. After I had heard these viewpoints, everything was changed according to their advice.

Recalling the circumstances of the writing of this drama over the past two years, I feel profoundly the importance of learning. The progression of my writing has been in every way a progression of learning. I learned some things from my friends in the drama circle, I learned some things from the specialists, and I learned some things from my non-specialist friends. Always, I was learning and seeking advice from every possible quarter.

This drama is far from sophisticated. The ideological form and content are still very much lacking. However, even speaking just on the basis of the progress of my own writing, there is one thing of which I am sure. That is simply that there is no need for us to fear things which we do not understand. As long as one is not afraid and is willing to go right to the root of a thing, then he can come to more or less understand it. On the other hand, the more one fears a thing, the more he cannot understand it, to the point where he will never understand it. However it happened, my knowledge of Peking Opera, after the learning process involved in writing this drama, has somewhat increased over what it was two years ago. My cultural level has been somewhat raised. The boundary between the dilettante and the expert is not impenetrable, but something which can be shattered. Speaking from my experience, it not only can be, but must be shattered.

Dare to think, dare to speak, and dare to do has been the new style since the Great Leap Forward. I wrote a drama. Thus I belong in the ranks of those who dare. If I did not dare, then I simply could not do anything successfully. As long as I dare, I can always more or less handle a thing. As for the magnitude of the achievement, or whether it is a success or failure, that is another thing. The historical development of a human society is also simply the history of people who dare to think, dare to speak, and dare to do. The ancients had a proverb, "Throw a brick to get a gem."[8] That is to say that this drama should be taken as "the throwing of a brick" to stimulate the interest of my friends in the field of history. Perhaps they will all come forward and write a new historical drama!

I also wish to clear up something else. After *Hai Jui's Dismissal* had been performed, there were a good many friends who urged me to write yet another play. Regarding this, I would like to say that one mistake is bad enough, but to repeat it?! I have absolutely no ambition or resolve to become a playwright. This is something I want to make clear once and for all.

Just for the understanding of the reader, two supplements have been added to this volume. One is a portrait of Hai Jui and a sample of his calligraphy, and one is a note concerning the historical records on which this drama is based.[9]

The portrait used is one displayed in the Chinese Historical Museum. Of the calligraphy, part was sent by comrade K'a Hui-hsin in Tientsin, and part was sent by comrade Ch'ang Jen-hsieh in Peking. I extend my thanks to both of them.

This is intended as an introduction.

Peitaiho, August 8, 1961

9

Introduction

Hai Jui (1515-87), whose courtesy name was Kang-feng, was a native of Kwangtung Chiunchou (now known as Hainan Island). In temperament he was resolute and in matters of principle he was steadfast. He was a famous, honest, and good official of the Ming Dynasty.

He opposed graft and extravagance. He advocated the use of heavy penalties to punish graft severely, and he established a clean and honest political climate. He advocated frugality in the allocation of financial resources, strictly implemented the regulations and policies of the government, and restrained oppressive landlords. He advocated and implemented the "single whip policy"[10] in order to mitigate the hardships of the impoverished. In addition, he expended great energy in repairing the irrigation system and decreasing the burden of petty irregular taxes. He took the disposition of court cases very seriously and he redressed injustices. He opposed evil and corrupt officials as well as the tyrannical gentry. However, he was also a loyal minister for the feudal ruling class, and his every political action stemmed from the motive of reinforcing the long-range interests of this feudal ruling class. Although he scolded the emperor and was imprisoned for it, indeed expected to be killed, when the emperor died, Hai Jui was moved to great weeping.

The people of the period liked him and sang his praises. The powerful officials, great landlords, and the gentry opposed him, denounced him, and closed ranks against him. But there was also a group of principled officials and young intelligentsia who supported him.

What I have written about in this play is just one episode during the time when he held the post of Ying T'ien Governor (at that time generally called Governor of Kiangnan). The time span runs from June of 1569 to January of 1570, seven months in all. In this year Hai Jui was fifty-four years of age.

The location is in Soochow, at that time the residence of the Ying T'ien Governor. The Ying T'ien Governor was in charge of the ten prefectures of Ying T'ien (Nanking), Soochow, Ch'ang-chow, Chinkiang, Sungkiang, Hweichow, T'ai-p'ing, Ningkuo, Anking, and Ch'ih-chow, as well as Kwangtechow. Moreover, he was simultaneously responsible for the grain tax in the three West Chekiang prefectures of Hangchow, Chia-hsing, and Huchow. The official duties of the governor were, first, to administer the government of the peoples; second, to superintend the grain reserves; third, to exercise control over the armed forces; fourth, to impeach government officials.

10

The hero of this play is Hai Jui. Opposing him are the retired prime minister, Hsü Chieh, and the group of officials and landlords represented by him. This group was collectively known as the gentry during the Ming Dynasty. (In the Ming Dynasty, those in the service of the court were called officials; after they had been dismissed from office and were living a life of leisure at home, they were called gentry. Such people were all big landlords with wealth and influence. Other terms used for them were *hsiang-shen, shen-chin, shen-fu,* etc., but in a word, they were all official-landlords.

This is the setting of the story. Hsü Chieh's third son, Hsü Ying, has used his position to antagonize the people and seize their fields, and he has harassed to death the only son of the peasant Chao Yü-shan. On top of all this, at the time of the Ch'ing-ming Festival he kidnaps Chao Yü-shan's granddaughter, Chao Hsiao-lan, and gives Chao Yü-shan a vicious beating. Chao Hsiao-lan's mother, Hung A-lan, lodges a complaint with the county court. The county magistrate, Wang Ming-yu, is secretly protecting the Hsü family, and will not hear the case. Hsü Ying buys off Wang Ming-yu and the Sungkiang Prefect and orders his servant, Hsü Fu, to go to court and testify that Hsü Ying had not gone out of the city at the time of the Ch'ing-ming Festival. Wang Ming-yu publicly beats Chao Yü-shan to death and drives out Hung A-lan, winding up the case. This vividly describes the sinister decadence of politics in the feudal era, the tyranny of the gentry, and the wretched circumstances, slavery, and oppression of the people.

Hai Jui comes to his post in ordinary clothes and on the way he learns directly from Hung A-lan and the masses of the peasants about the case of Hsü Ying and about the circumstances of the local people whose land is being usurped by the gentry.

Hai Jui pays a visit to Hsü Chieh. Hsü Chieh advises him that he ought to uphold the law strictly, meting out the same treatment to prince and commoner alike. The gist of his comments is that he wants Hai Jui to restrain with a heavy hand the frivolous lawsuits of the "wicked people" and protect the privileges of the gentry. Hai Jui brings up the case of Hung A-lan, but Hsü Chieh lies right to the end. Moreover, he instigates Hsü Ying to have Hsü Fu pose as a *hsiu-ts'ai* [11] and go to the court to give evidence.

Hai Jui is unalterably opposed to injustice and he orders the gentry to return the lands they have seized from the common people. When he discusses these measures with the members of his family, his mother agrees with the utmost vigour. This strengthens his resolve still further.

In the scene where the case is settled, Hai Jui exposes the false testimony of the Hsü family's bondsman and punishes him according to law. He also disposes of the avaricious and corrupt officials.

11

Hsü Ying is sentenced to death, and Hsü Chieh pays a personal visit to Hai Jui. He talks about their past friendship and begs for lenient treatment. Hai Jui ignores all this and justly repudiates him, thus initiating an open struggle. Hsü Chieh offers to atone for his son's crime by returning the land, but Hai Jui sternly points out that the lands which have been snatched from the people will be returned in any case and Hsü Ying, having violated the law, has to be punished. Hsü Chieh then goes so far as to threaten him, saying that he could lose his office by committing this kind of transgression against the gentry. Hai Jui is still unmoved. Finally they break off their friendship and Hsü Chieh leaves in a rage.

Hsü Chieh does not willingly accept defeat. He holds a secret meeting with his close friends in order to plan a counter-attack. They send people to the capital city to bribe the eunuchs and the court officials so that Hai Jui will be dismissed from office. The new governor, Tai Feng-hsiang, comes to take up his post immediately. Hai Jui has already received the execution order for the two criminals, Hsü Ying and Wang Ming-yu, who had been sentenced at the Fall Assizes, but Tai Feng-hsiang tries every kind of browbeating to dissuade him from carrying out the sentences. Hai Jui is immovable. He orders that the sentences be carried out first; only then will he hand over his credentials and seal of office and retire from public life.

The Tai Feng-hsiang in the play is the man who impeached Hai Jui and had him dismissed. He was a spokesman for the Kiangnan gentry at court. Here, just for the sake of convenience, we have him replacing Hai Jui as Ying T'ien Governor.

This play emphasizes Hai Jui's uprightness of character. He would not submit to the fierce and overbearing, he was not scared off by failure, and when he did fail, he tried again with a relentless will. What is expressed is the internal struggle of the feudal ruling class, a struggle between the left faction of Hai Jui and the right faction, that of the clique of officials and landlords which took Hsü Chieh as its leader. Hai Jui was a loyal minister of the feudal ruling class, but he was comparatively far-sighted, and comparatively close to the people. For the long-range benefit of his own class, he advocated doing some good things which were beneficial for the people of the times. He restricted the gentry's lawless fleecing of the peasantry. He impinged on the interests of the right faction of his own class and opened up a violent struggle. During the struggle in this last act, Hai Jui loses office, but he absolutely refuses to yield an inch. Because he did some good things, the people of that era supported him and sang his praises. Hai Jui's position in history ought to be recognized. Some of his good actions and virtues also deserve our study today.

November 13, 1960 – seventh draft
August 8, 1961, final revision at Peitaho

HAI JUI'S DISMISSAL
An Historical Drama

Time The season of the Ch'ing-ming Festival,[12] 1569.
Place Below Heng Yün Mountain in Hua-t'ing County, Sungkiang Prefecture.
Characters Hsü Chieh's third son, HSÜ YING, about forty years old, a powerful lord
and an evil tyrant.
The peasant CHAO YÜ-SHAN, sixty-five years old.
Chao's daughter-in-law, HUNG A-LAN, thirty-five years old.
CHAO HSIAO-LAN, Chao Yü-shan's granddaughter, sixteen years old.
WANG MING-YU, the Hua-t'ing District Magistrate, an avaricious official,
forty years old.
A crowd of Hsü family bondsmen, a group of Hua-t'ing County yamen
runners, and a great number of common people filing complaints.
A crowd of country people.

Enter Hsü Ying, riding a horse, amid a great crowd of male slaves.

HSÜ YING *recites*
The colours of spring fill the frontiers beyond the city.
I wander leisurely,
occupied with my gold stirrup and riding baton.
I ride swiftly.
Let me gaze on all the many and varied flowers.
Ai ya!
There are some pretty ones over there –
let us go after them.

I am Hsü Ying, the third master of the Hsü family. Pretending to visit
ancestral graves, I have come here to amuse myself. I shall pull a fast
one! How delightful it is going to be! When one suddenly sees before
him two very attractive and seductive girls among the graves, why not
go ahead and have some fun with them? Let us go quickly, little ones!
exits

*Enter Hung A-lan and Chao Hsiao-lan, holding incense and paper
money.*

HUNG A-LAN *sings*
At Ch'ing-ming Festival time
we sweep the new grave and burn paper money.
I ache with sorrow
for the death of my husband one year ago.
Despite the profusion of flowers and willows,
I have no heart for pleasure.
My father-in-law is old,

14

my daughter weak and helpless.
Who will take pity on us?

Hsiao-lan, light the incense and burn the money in respect for your father. *Mother and daughter pray together, crying.* Oh, father of Hsiao-lan!

continues song

Your family depended solely on you
to sow the grain and plough the fields,
by stars of morning and by moon at night,
rising early and retiring late,
raising cattle, tending mulberry and hemp,
slaving the year long,
paying exorbitant taxes, living a hard life,
enduring all kinds of harassment.
As things progressed in this way,
the sky suddenly fell in on us.
The Hsü family antedated the mortgage on our land.
They seized our crops and produce
and still demanded taxes on our land.
We wore our shoes out going to the magistrate
and pleading with the gentry.
You were so angry you spat blood
and fell sick from bitter hatred.
In just a few months you died.
We buried you before the mountain.

Oh, God, father of Hsiao-lan, what are your wife and daughter to do for the rest of our lives? When will the injustice you received ever be redressed?

CHAO[13] HSIAO-LAN Do not cry, mother. There are some people coming over there.

Mother and daughter tidy up their sacrificial baskets and bowls and prepare to leave. Hsü Ying comes onstage, amid a crowd of attendants. Hsü Ying tries to flirt with Chao Hsiao-lan, but Hsiao-lan avoids him and Hung A-lan stands in his way.

HSÜ YING Go away, go away! She is the one I want, not you.

HUNG A-LAN The young gentleman should show a little respect. She is my daughter.

HSÜ YING That's wonderful. You may as well both go to my house together.

15

HUNG A-LAN   This is a little strange. We are neither relatives nor close friends. What would we do at your house?

HSÜ YING   All you will do is be my concubines, and I guarantee that both of you will have more food than you can eat and more clothes than you can wear.

HUNG A-LAN   Nothing doing. Hsiao-lan, let us go quickly.

Hsü Ying directs his servants to block their way.

HUNG A-LAN   In broad daylight the women of decent families are molested. Fellow peasants, help!

HSÜ YING   Don't raise a hue and cry over nothing. I, the third master of the Hsü family, would be incapable of mistreating you two young women.

HUNG A-LAN   What?! Third Master Hsü is the enemy who killed my husband! Help! Help!

Hearing her voice a large group of peasants comes on stage. Hung A-lan and her daughter take the opportunity to escape.

GROUP OF
PEASANTS   It's that rotten egg from the Hsü family abusing people again! Why does God in Heaven not open his eyes and punish this rotten egg, eh? It's outrageous!

HSÜ YING   Go after them – fast!

The peasant masses are driven off and Hsü Ying and his bondsmen pursue them offstage. Hung A-lan, Chao Hsiao-lan, and Chao Yü-shan come on separately. They meet. Hsü Ying returns with his group of bondsmen and Chao Yü-shan steps in front of them, blocking their way.

HSÜ YING   Don't go. Let us talk it over.

CHAO YÜ-SHAN   Talk what over? Third Master Hsü, your family has usurped my family's land and hounded to death the only son I raised. And you still want to compel an old man to pay taxes and run errands. But even this is not enough for you. You still have to come and insult and ridicule the widow and orphan[14] in my family. You simply will not allow people to go on living!

HSÜ YING   Chao Yü-shan, do you not know your place? Considering that a

16

CHAO YÜ-SHAN   poor old man like you certainly cannot support them, you had better listen to me. They would wear silk and satin, have maids at their beck and call, and have more of everything than they can use. I would also reward you, old man, with some rice to eat.

CHAO YÜ-SHAN   What? Stop this talk! Hsü Ying, I am a poor man but there is nothing poor about my spirit! And I do not deal in human beings. Get out of here fast! Be off with you!

HSÜ YING   He is truly too ignorant to appreciate the kindness I am showing him. Little ones, take them by force!

Hsü Fu and a large group of bond slaves drag off Chao Hsiao-lan while Chao Yü-shan and Hung A-lan try to obstruct them.

HSÜ YING   Beat him, beat this corpse which is too stupid to lie down.

The bondsmen of the Hsü family give Chao Yü-shan a painful beating, while Hung A-lan and Chao Hsiao-lan try to save him. Chao Yü-shan is beaten into a stupor and Hsü Ying leads his bond slaves in carrying off Hsiao-lan.

CROWD OF
PEASANTS   Plundering, carrying off the women of decent families, and beating the life out of men in broad daylight. What kind of world is this? Where is the law? Where is justice?

Hung A-lan weeps bitterly. All the peasants attend to Chao Yü-shan as best they can, and Chao gradually regains consciousness.

CHAO YÜ-SHAN   Daughter-in-law, this is no time for crying. The important thing now is to go quickly to the district office, file a complaint, and see that granddaughter is rescued and brought back to us.
sings
In their tyrannical treatment of other people
they rival the tiger and wolf.
In order to redress our grievances,
we must go and report them in court.
As long as the law of the court endures,
its function should be
to redress the grievances of wronged people.

HUNG A-LAN   My father-in-law's wounds are serious and there is no one to tend to you. Your daughter-in-law cannot go.

PEASANTS   Young lady, concern yourself only with going and laying the charges.

17

Your father-in-law has us to stay behind and look after him. Put your mind at ease and go!

HUNG A-LAN If this is the case, all I can do is thank you. Father-in-law, I am on my way.

CHAO YÜ-SHAN Hurry there and hurry back; rescue my granddaughter.

HUNG A-LAN I shall. *exits*

Exit the large group of peasants, supporting Chao Yü-shan.

SCENE 1A In court

A large group of runners crowds onstage with the Hua-t'ing Magistrate, Wang Ming-yu. The commoners who are pressing suits then follow.

WANG MING-YU *recites*
I am a seventh grade magistrate.
But what use are essays in the work of an official?
When I see gold and silver, my mouth waters.
The surname of a person matters not to me.
Just so long as he sends me money,
he will win even against my own parents.
Though the basis of his case be sound,
if he has no money, there is no use discussing it!

What! Are all these people here before us laying complaints?

PLAINTIFFS We are all filing charges.

They hand up the documents pertaining to their accusations.

WANG MING-YU Who are you accusing?

FIRST PLAINTIFF I am accusing the family of Grand Tutor Hsü of seizing people's land.

SECOND PLAINTIFF I report that the family of Grand Tutor Hsü has been appropriating other people's property.

THIRD PLAINTIFF I report that Third Master Hsü has been seizing people's houses.

18

WANG MING-YU That is strange. Ever since I came to this post, I have had people coming every day to report the Hsü family. Again today, every one of them is reporting the Hsü family. They all report this one family and even the causes of their complaints are identical; it is always because they are stealing people's property. They really make a fuss over nothing. Do you think the Grand Tutor is someone whom you may accuse like this? I have long heard that the people of this area are by nature of a wicked and arrogant character. It is really true, indeed it is! You really are wicked people; you really are wicked, aren't you? Attendants, drive these wicked people out!

The runners drive the common people offstage. Hung A-lan comes on and sounds the drum, and the runners beckon her to enter and kneel down.

WANG MING-YU Here comes another plaintiff. I can guess, without a doubt, she is here to complain about the Hsü family. Well, all right, woman, whom are you accusing?

HUNG A-LAN Your Worship, I accuse Third Master Hsü of kidnapping my daughter and administering a beating to my father-in-law which resulted in serious injury. I trust Your Worship will redress my grievance! *weeps*

WANG MING-YU I was able to divine her intentions as well as if I were God himself. Well! What about your daughter?

HUNG A-LAN She has been kidnapped by Third Master Hsü.

WANG MING-YU Who will testify to that effect?

HUNG A-LAN There were many of my fellow peasants who saw it with their own eyes.

WANG MING-YU Where are these witnesses?

HUNG A-LAN My father-in-law was severely injured. All our good peasant friends are at home looking after him and so they have not come.

WANG MING-YU I knew from the beginning you were going to pull a stunt like this. First no evidence and then no witnesses. Who really took your daughter? Where is your father-in-law?

HUNG A-LAN He was so badly injured that he cannot even move.

19

WANG MING-YU Enough! If you are going to make accusations concerning injuries, you must verify the injuries. That is the universal requirement. If your father-in-law does not come to verify his injuries, how am I to know whether he has any injuries or not? You come here to launch a suit and in the first place you do not have formal papers. In the second place, you have no relevant evidence; and third, you have no proof of injury. This is obviously the false report of a vicious person. I am taking into consideration the fact that you are a woman and that this is your first offence, so I am not going to deal with you severely. Come, take her out of here.

HUNG A-LAN I have been badly mistreated. Your Worship, please have compassion, and redress my grievances.

WANG MING-YU If there is any injustice, it will be set right, but the making of false accusations must also be dealt with. If you are going to file a complaint, you must have people to come as witnesses and give evidence. The only proof is what I hear from your mouth alone. I am not the type of addle-brained official who is going to hear one side of the story only and believe it.

HUNG A-LAN Your Worship is an honest official. He should redress my grievance.

WANG MING-YU Of course I am an honest official. What need is there for you to say that? If you are not satisfied, next time come back with witnesses to testify for you. Now leave the court.

Exit the runners. Exit Hung A-lan, weeping.

WANG MING-YU This is a bothersome case to handle. Both kidnapping and beating people. Supposing I were to handle it according to law, could a little minion like me afford to provoke the wrath of Grand Tutor Hsü? Yet if I let it drag on without doing anything, this woman can come here every day laying charges and bother me to death. So how am I to handle it? *ponders* I know, I shall personally go and consult with His Excellency Li P'ing-tu, the Prefect. He is extremely knowledgeable and he will have a way of dealing with it.

Night and day, the wicked people stir up wind and waves,
When shall we ever see the end of the annoyances they cause?
exits

SCENE 2 The case is tried

Time   One month later.
Place   The yamen of the Hua-t'ing Magistrate.
Characters HSÜ YING and HSÜ FU.
           The farmer CHAO YÜ-SHAN and HUNG A-LAN.
           The Hua-t'ing Magistrate WANG MING-YU, in the company of many
           runners.
           A crowd of peasants.

Hsü Ying and Hsü Fu come onstage.

HSÜ YING *recites*
           I have sent gold and profferred flatteries,
           and I still have some tricks up my sleeve
           to win this case.

           My good Chao Yü-shan, I did not think you would dare to come into
           court and report me. However, one must fight fire with fire, and I did
           not have to think long before a scheme occurred to me. I sent Hsü Fu
           with two hundred taels of gold for the magistrate and three hundred
           taels for the prefect. I have bought off everyone concerned, at all
           levels. That Wang Ming-yu is an exceptionally astute fellow. He says
           it would be absolutely lacking in propriety on his part if he were not
           to deal severely with any wicked people who make false accusations
           against the gentry. So there is to be a lawsuit, eh Chao Yü-shan? We
           shall see how far you are prepared to carry your evil scheme! Hsü Fu!

HSÜ FU Yes?

HSÜ YING Go into the court, and if the magistrate asks you what happened on
           that day, you must be very careful; we cannot let the cat out of the
           bag.

HSÜ FU That goes without saying. You may rest assured, Master. *They exit
           together.*

           Wang Ming-yu comes on, followed by the runners, and takes his seat.

WANG MING-YU *recites*
           These last few days have seen much good fortune.
           How much has greased my palm, I do not know.
           Concerning lawsuits, the money involved is my only interest,
           yet my reputation surpasses that of Pao Lao.[15]

21

This is really very interesting, very interesting! It used to be that I knew only how to fleece the poor. But there is no percentage in that. Today, for instance, even the family of the Grand Tutor Hsü has sent great quantities of gold. Being an official has really been worthwhile for me. In any event, I must bring this case to a close today. If I don't, people will say that I am a bumbling official for not even being able to handle a small affair like this. Runners, call into court the people involved in the case of Hung A-lan.

The runners shout out the summons. Enter Hung A-lan, Chao Yü-shan, and a crowd of peasants.

ALL　We simple folk and this young lady wish to pay our respects to Your Worship.

WANG MING-YU　Stand to one side. These last few days I have been conducting thorough investigations into the case of Hung A-lan. Today I am holding court. You must speak only the facts. You must not add anything extra in order to try and make trouble. Hung A-lan.

HUNG A-LAN　I am here.

WANG MING-YU　You accuse Hsü Ying of kidnapping your daughter; what day did this kidnapping take place?

HUNG A-LAN　He kidnapped her on the day of the Ch'ing-ming Festival.

WANG MING-YU　Are there any eyewitnesses or not?

ALL THE
PEASANTS　We humble people saw it with our own eyes.

WANG MING-YU　Hung A-lan, you accuse Hsü Ying of beating your father-in-law. Has your father-in-law come or not?

CHAO YÜ-SHAN　I am here.

WANG MING-YU　Where are the injuries you suffered in the beating?

CHAO YÜ-SHAN　They beat me with their fists and kicked me with their feet. I was injured all over my body.

WANG MING-YU　Do you have an eyewitness or not?

22

ALL THE PEASANTS We folk saw it with our own eyes.

WANG MING-YU Coroner, verify these injuries.

The coroner strips off Chao Yü-shan's clothing in order to examine the wounds.

CORONER I must report, Your Worship, that his body is entirely unmarked. There are no scabs or scars and there are no injuries.

WANG MING-YU So! The colossal gall of you vicious people! You spread slanders and false accusations. Bring the cane and give him a severe beating for me.

CHAO YÜ-SHAN Eh? Your Worship, my body *does* have wounds and scars. How can it be said that there are no wounds? I beg Your Worship to make a careful examination.

PEASANTS Chao Yü-shan took a fearsome beating at the hands of Hsü Ying; this we saw with our own eyes. If this be false, we are willing to take the punishment ourselves.

WANG MING-YU This is certainly very strange. There clearly are not any wounds, yet the whole lot of you says that there are. Coroner, go and have another look and tell me what you find.

CORONER There appear to be some self-inflicted wounds here, resulting from an intentional fall. But there are absolutely no traces of any injuries resulting from a beating.

WANG MING-YU Runner, summon Hsü Ying into court.

Enter Hsü Ying and Hsü Fu

HSÜ YING Hsü Ying, of the Hsü family of gentry, wishes to pay his respects to Your Worship.

WANG MING-YU Do not stand on ceremony. Hsü Ying, we have on hand here some people who accuse you of kidnapping a young girl and cruelly beating a respectable man. Can there be anything to such a story?

HSÜ YING I am a member of the Prime Minister's household. I spend my time earnestly studying the classics and I thoroughly understand the lofty ideas expressed in them. How could I stoop to kidnapping girls and cruelly beating respectable folk? Your Worship understands clearly

23

what I mean. Your Worship, may I inquire on what day this took place?

WANG MING-YU   According to the original accusation, it was on the day of the Ch'ing-ming Festival.

HSÜ YING   The Ch'ing-ming Festival? Where did I go on that day? Oh! I know! It was that day that I was at the home of Scholar Chang,[16] discussing the classics. I never went out of the city.

WANG MING-YU   Where are your witnesses?

HSÜ YING   My bond slave Hsü Fu went along and was in attendance. He can bear witness.

WANG MING-YU   Hsü Fu, where did Hsü Ying go on the day of the Ch'ing-ming Festival?

HSÜ FU   I can report to Your Worship that on the day of the Ch'ing-ming Festival the third master was indeed studying at the home of a *hsiu-ts'ai*[17] of this city, and he never left the city. The family bondsmen were at his side and I can testify that we never left him for a single moment.

WANG MING-YU   Then this is the way it was. On the day of the Ch'ing-ming Festival, Hsü Ying spent the whole day studying at the home of a *hsiu-ts'ai* in this city. If this is so, could he then have split himself in two so as to go outside the city, kidnapping and beating people? This is very obviously a case of wicked people making false accusations against gentry. This is absolutely intolerable. Come forward, attendants, and give Hung A-lan a severe beating!

HUNG A-LAN   Your Worship! If I must repeat it a million times, this business of kidnapping and beating people is true, it is absolutely accurate. I have the peasants of my neighbourhood here as witnesses. Your Worship must see that justice is done for me. My daughter is now in the Hsü household. I beg Your Worship to return her to us so that flesh and blood might dwell together again.

WANG MING-YU   What! The great gall of this shrew! So you have witnesses. Am I therefore to act as if the others do not have witnesses? Am I to be so partial as to simply assume that your witnesses are telling the truth and that the other party's witnesses are lying? His Worship hears both sides and then decides according to law. To listen to one side

24

only would be very poor justice. If I did not listen to what the gentry said, how could I possibly listen to the words of poor people on the other hand? Come, drag her out and give her a sound thrashing.

CHAO YÜ-SHAN   Have mercy, Your Worship. Although I am involved only in farming and am a very poor man, my human spirit is not poor at all. Although I do not read books, I do nevertheless possess some intelligence. I inherited a little property and my whole family depended on this for a living. Third Master Hsü forged a contract, antedated it, and seized my land as his own. Because of this, my only son became so vexed and angry that he died of chagrin, leaving his widow and child. The land was gone, but the taxes still had to be paid. I had to pay the grain tax by doing corvée labour. There was no place where I could go to report these injustices. On that day of the Ch'ing-ming Festival, Third Master Hsü, thinking he could get away with it because of his position, kidnapped my granddaughter and gave me a severe beating, leaving me wounded. And so I have suffered one wrong after another. Overhead is the sun in the sky and here below are my peasant neighbours; and all can corroborate what I say. If Your Worship will not do anything about it for us, but on the contrary believes only the stories of our opponent and wants to beat the plaintiff, where are the eternal principles of justice? Where is your conscience? Your Worship, you cannot behave like this; you must act in the interests of the little people!

WANG MING-YU   The great gall of you wicked people! It is absolutely clear that you have no wounds yet you still say that you were wounded. It is absolutely clear that the other party was at the home of a friend, studying, and never went out, yet you falsely accuse him of going out into the countryside, beating and kidnapping. Is this your universal principle of justice? Is this an example of conscience? Your human spirit is also poor, so poor that in the end the only thing you can think of is to summon up all your gall and make false accusations against the gentry. You are truly an extremely vicious and evil man! Come, take him out and thrash him!

CHAO YÜ-SHAN   Your Worship, you cannot beat me! If you are really going to have me beaten, I am going to report it.

WANG MING-YU   Where are you going to report it?

CHAO YÜ-SHAN   I shall report in the prefectural court; I shall report it in Soochow; I shall report it in the capital:

25

sings
When an old man like me suffers injustices,
high Heaven sees.
Streams of tears flow for my beaten body
and my kidnapped granddaughter.
Your office is used not to uphold justice for the people,
but to transgress it.
I shall charge you in the capital
as a corrupt official, selling law for the highest bribe.

WANG MING-YU The nerve of you!
sings
I never knew the wicked people
could really be so bold and daring
as to accuse the gentry falsely
in such a wild and thoughtless manner.
Come, seize him, let his punishment
be eighty strokes of the bamboo.

Give him a fierce and thorough beating for me!

*The runners drag Chao Yü-shan out to receive the heavy beating and
Chao Yü-shan is beaten to death.*

RUNNERS *returning* Your Worship, we must report that the guilty man has died
from the beating.

HUNG A-LAN My God, no!
sings
With a heart full of grief and anger,
I can only call on God in Heaven.
When my father-in-law can be beaten to death
right before the court,
who among men can still distinguish right from wrong?
Heaven, oh heaven!
My daughter who was kidnapped remains in danger.

WANG MING-YU *Alarmed, pales and becomes upset, but then settles down.* Carry him
out and get her out of the court.

*Exit the group of peasants, carrying Chao Yü-shan's corpse. Exit
Hung A-lan, weeping bitterly. Exit Hsü Ying, laughing, followed by
Hsü Fu, who is scowling.*

WANG MING-YU We have been careless. I did not think this old fellow was so unable

26

to stand a beating. *ponders* Still, this is nothing to worry about, nothing to worry about at all!

Enter a runner to deliver the Peking Gazette.

RUNNER   Your Worship, I have here an urgent dispatch. Please read it, Your Worship.

WANG MING-YU   *Tears it open and reads it carefully; gives a start and nervously drops the paper.* Good Lord! Hai Jui has been taken from his position as Censor in the Supreme Court and is ordered to take the post of Governor of Ying T'ien and the Ten Prefectures. My God! This old beggar is going nowhere else but right here to Kiangnan. What are we to do now? *He has dropped the Peking Gazette. Now he picks it up again, hesitatingly.*

RUNNER   What? Hai Ch'ing-t'ien[18] is coming? What can we do?

WANG MING-YU   Get my luggage ready. We leave on a journey to Soochow immediately.

The runner accompanies Wang Ming-yu offstage.

SCENE 3 Taking office

Time   The first week in June, 1569.
Place   The pavilion for welcoming officials, outside Chang Men,[19] in Soochow.
Characters The Prefect of Soochow, CHENG YÜ, fifty-five years of age, willing to
            enact his duties honestly. He has a good reputation as an official.
            The Magistrate of Wu Hsien,[20] HSIAO YEN, forty-five years of age, an
            avaricious official.
            The Sungkiang Prefect, LI P'ING-TU, approximately fifty years old,
            sycophant of the gentry. Prone to bend the law to increase his own
            wealth, he is widely known as Li Po-p'i.[21]
            The Hua-t'ing Magistrate, WANG MING-YU.
            HUNG A-LAN and the group of peasants.
            HAI JUI, fifty-four years old, beard already half whitened, wearing
            ordinary, everyday attire.
            Hai Jui's mother, HSIEH SHIH, seventy-one years old, of stern and
            upright disposition. Since her husband died while she was still in her
            youth, she alone has educated Hai Jui and raised him to manhood.
            Hai Jui has the utmost respect for her.
            Hai Jui's wife, WANG SHIH. She is his second wife. She is thirty years
            of age and of a meek and timid disposition. She greatly respects Hai
            Jui but also fears that his unbending principles will bring misfortune.
            She often advises him against doing things, but after he explains his
            reasoning to her, she fully supports him.
            HAI P'ENG, the aged servant of the Hai family. He is resolute, loyal,
            and sincere, but fearful that Hai Jui will offend someone. He too
            tries to dissuade Hai Jui at times. He is fully devoted to his master.
            Also, he suffers from contradictions, but in the end he is always
            straightened out by Hai Jui.
            An officer, and a great many soldiers.

*Enter a group of officials, officers, and soldiers, accompanied by
banners, parasols, and shouting.*

CHENG YÜ Gentlemen, Censor Hai has already started on his journey from Nan-
          king, but to date he has still not arrived. I fear this will be yet another
          fruitless trip on our part.

HSIAO YEN When the eunuch Huang Chin, superintendent of the Imperial Silk
           Factory, heard that Hai Jui was coming, the old man's big sedan
           chair was reduced from eight to four men.

LI P'ING-TU   Yes. And we have some gentry right here who have gone out at
              night and smeared black paint over the red gates in order to avoid
              any unnecessary trouble.[22]

WANG MING-YU Gentlemen, everyone describes Hai Jui as an absolutely honest and
              upright official, but when all is said and done, what kind of man is
              he?

CHENG YÜ   When I was in the capital many years ago, I knew a little about what
              kind of man Censor Hai was. Gentlemen, I shall give you a bit of a
              description:
              sings
              Recognized as the most upright of men,
              he gave himself the name Kang-feng.[23]
              Near the close of the Chia Ching Reign[24]
              he memorialized the throne,
              provoking the emperor's wrath.
              He tried to persuade the emperor the pursuit
              of immortality was wasted effort:
              "Whether we speak of ancient times or modern,
              was there ever a man who never died?
              If one squanders wealth on sacrifices
              while the affairs of the people are neglected,
              the people will all complain,
              and war, poverty, and distress
              arise from all directions.
              Now the people use 'Chia Ching' to signify
              'every house is empty.'[25]
              Unless a change is made,
              the state will be endangered; you
              will then not dare to face your ancestors."

He scolded the emperor bitterly and the emperor flew into a great
rage. He was going to condemn Hai Jui to death. He ordered some
men to apprehend him and not let him escape. Afterwards it became
known that Hai Jui had already put his last affairs in order, and the
emperor was so taken aback he did not know what to do. Hai Jui
was locked up in the Imperial Prison and endured all sorts of punishments. Only when the emperor died was he pardoned and let out of
prison. Now that he is coming to Kiangnan, gentlemen, you will have
to watch your steps.

*Hsiao Yen, Li P'ing-tu, and Wang Ming-yu pale and become very
nervous and jumpy.*

29

CHENG YÜ The weather is absolutely scorching. Let us now take a little rest in the Official Welcoming Pavilion. When the heralds arrive, we shall come back out to welcome him. That will be soon enough. Come, let us go back to the pavilion.

All exit together.

HAI JUI *offstage* Let us hurry forward.

Enter Hai Jui, Hsieh Shih, Wang Shih, and Hai P'eng, together.

HAI JUI *sings*
I have imperial orders
to tour the Ten Prefectures,
first to Chin-chang.
This will allow me to fulfil
my ambition to help the weak
against the strong.
Kiangnan is a place of rice and fish,
but the land tax there is high.
It is often said that above there is heaven,
while below there is Su-Hang.[26]
But evil gentry and extortionate officials
tyrannize their fellow countrymen;
so badly do they use the people
that many of the suffering have fled.
People are poor, there is no money, and
the lifeblood of the country is drying up.
I, Hai Jui, if I will serve my emperor,
must take these matters into my own hands.

WANG SHIH The perspiration is flowing like rain right through my clothes. Although the scenery is very pretty, I simply cannot enjoy it.

HSIEH SHIH Son, how far do we still have to go from here to the city of Soochow?

HAI JUI We go directly ahead, not much farther, and then we are at Soochow City. The weather is scorching hot. Mother, how about resting for fifteen minutes or so and then going on?

HSIEH SHIH Just as you say.

HAI JUI Look, up ahead there is a grove of trees. Please, mother, have a rest there. Hai P'eng, lead the way.

Exit Hsieh Shih, Wang Shih, and Hai P'eng.

30

Enter Hung A-lan and a crowd of peasants.

THIRD
PEASANT   The weather is scorching hot. Let us have a little rest before going on, eh? Good lady, you are crying and sobbing so uncontrollably, what has been done to you?

HUNG A-LAN   I am going to Soochow to launch a complaint at the governor's yamen.

THIRD
PEASANT   Whom are you filing your complaint against?

HUNG A-LAN   I am going to file against the third son of the Hsü family in Hua-t'ing County and against the Hua-t'ing Magistrate for seizing land, kidnapping, and murder.

THIRD
PEASANT   Please tell us a few details about the case.

HUNG A-LAN   Ah, me! Heaven help me!
               sings
               The evil Hsü Ying tramples on our rights,
               using his power to seize our land.
               Old men are beaten to death, girls kidnapped,
               and I am driven to beseech Heaven.
               The Hua-t'ing Magistrate shielded the defendant
               and put the blame on me.
               With an anxious heart I rush to Soochow
               to report these things to the governor.

               Hai Jui listens attentively, shaking his head.

THIRD
PEASANT   Can it really be true that there are injustices such as these?

FIRST
PEASANT   How can it be untrue? We all saw it with our own eyes.
               sings
               In an old grave and a new one are buried
               father and son, two generations,
               A son hounded to death, his father
               beaten to death, his daughter kidnapped.
               Buried in this ground will be
               the injustices of three generations.

HAI JUI   Why do you not go and report it to the officials?

SECOND
PEASANT   Excuse me sir, but you would have no way of knowing how it could

31

be that we would not report such a thing. When it *was* reported, the injured person was beaten to death.

HAI JUI If this was the case, what law did they rely on for their judgment?

FIRST
PEASANT They said it was a false accusation, that he had falsely accused the gentry.

HAI JUI Why did they say it was a false accusation? Was there an eyewitness?

FIRST
PEASANT Yes, his family's head servant gave evidence.

HAI JUI What! How can a bond slave be a witness for his master? Well, what testimony did he give?

SECOND
PEASANT He said that on the day of the Ch'ing-ming Festival, Third Master Hsü spent the entire day reading at the home of a *hsiu-ts'ai* of this city, and what is more, that he never went outside the city.

HAI JUI What Third Master Hsü is that?

FIRST
PEASANT The Third Master Hsü of the family of Grand Tutor Hsü. Is there any other?

HAI JUI No, you are quite right. Since Third Master Hsü never went outside the city, how could he still be in the countryside kidnapping and beating people?

FIRST
PEASANT Bah! Do you think we were all seeing a ghost in broad daylight? We all watched him commit this kidnapping and beating with our own eyes.

HAI JUI Then it was your own fault. Since you saw it with your own eyes, why did you not go and give evidence?

SECOND
PEASANT Oh, sir,
sings
When we all go into court to appear as witnesses,
the magistrate grows rich on the bribes he receives.
The words of the gentry he believes absolutely,
but he has difficulty accepting
what poor men see with their own eyes.

HAI JUI The speech of the gentry is automatically true and the testimony of poor people is automatically false.

CROWD OF
PEASANTS Exactly.

HAI JUI In this case the gentry was only one man and there are many of you. When you had all had your say, did he still not believe you?

FIRST
PEASANT Sir, how could you know the sufferings and hardships of us poor people? We are all tenants of the Hsü family. How could we dare to say anything more?

HAI JUI Oh! You are all tenants of the Hsü Family.

ALL THE
PEASANTS Our lands and fields have all been seized by the Hsü family but we still have to hand over the rents and do corvée labour. Truly, we have a bitter time of it.

HAI JUI This is your own fault too. Why do you not report it?

FIRST
PEASANT Sir, you are not a local man, and so it is not surprising that you think the way you do. The prefect is the famous Li Po-p'i[27] and the magistrate is an absolutely corrupt official. How could we dare to lay a complaint?
sings
The yamens of the officials are opened wide,
but if you have only evidence and no money,
you stay outside.
From the highest levels to the lowest,
it is always an official's world,
and they say the poor have only themselves to blame
that they do not live better.

HAI JUI Amazing! But if you cannot report it to the prefect or the magistrate, where are you going now?

THIRD
PEASANT We are going to lay our complaint at the yamen of the Soochow Governor.

HAI JUI The Soochow Governor. Then does he not demand money, and can he see that justice is done for you?

THIRD
PEASANT Exactly. The newly appointed governor is Hai Ch'ing-t'ien, and he

33

certainly can see that justice is done for us. If you listen, I shall tell you about him.

sings

Many years ago
when I was selling rice in Shun-an,
everyone talked of the fairness and impartiality
of the official, Hai Ch'ing-t'ien.
He decreased the number of couriers
and implemented the "single whip policy."[28]
The mouths of the people are as tablets,
recording the merits of a good magistrate
and praising him.
He abolished the *li* headmen,[29]
removed some bad traditions,
instituted many good policies.
He encouraged the people in their farming,
regarding them as his own children,
and all who had previously fled returned.
Clothed in broadcloth, living only on vegetables,
he endured a very hard life.
He rounded up bullies, eliminated scoundrels,
saw justice done in court.
When he was transferred and had to leave,
the common people he had helped were very grieved.

HAI JUI   Do you truly believe that he can act on your behalf?

THIRD
PEASANT   Of course he still has not arrived to take up his post. We are just going by all the reports that say he lets the common people state their grievances and gets them redressed. But if he will not act for us, how can he still retain the name of Ch'ing-t'ien?

HAI JUI   I see. Thank you for your information.

Sound of drums and music from the rear.

SECOND
PEASANT   Here come the officials out to receive Hai Ch'ing-t'ien. Let us get a look at Hai Ch'ing-t'ien.

Hung A-lan and all the peasants push forward and collide head-on with the group of officials, officers, and soldiers. A soldier knocks the Third Peasant down; in helping him up, Hai Jui then bumps into Li P'ing-tu and both are knocked off balance.

34

LI P'ING-TU   You blind old fool, you knocked me over! Beat this old good-for-
nothing!

*A soldier raises his whip, Cheng Yü restrains him, and the crowd of
officials, officers, and soldiers goes off. Exit Hung A-lan and all the
peasants in a fright.*

HAI JUI   This petty little official with such an awe-inspiring reputation!
sings
The common people come in droves to lay their complaints.
Supporting their aged, leading young by the hand,
they flee to the remotest parts,
all because avaricious officials
behave no better than packs of foxes and dogs.
They squeeze and bleed the poor and proffer bribes
that work against the people's good.
This one uses his awesome reputation
to intimidate and push others around.
It is obviously his habit to treat others
with haughtiness and contempt.
As Governor of Kiangnan, Hai Jui
will nourish and protect
the interests of the masses.
I shall sweep
all these evil officials away,
repress the sinister, support the virtuous.

In a word:

I shall restore the fabric
of our society and destroy the tyrants.
I shall fulfil the ambitions I have cherished
through my entire life. *exits*

35

SCENE 4 Meeting with Hsü

Time   Ten days later.
Place   The mansion of Hsü Chieh in Hua-t'ing County.
Characters   HAI JUI, wearing a silk cap and long red robe.
   HAI P'ENG.
   HSÜ CHIEH, seventy-five years of age. His beard is streaked with white and grey. He is small, short in stature, with a fair complexion. He carries himself elegantly. Dressed in ordinary clothes.
   A domestic servant of the Hsü family.

Hsü Chieh enters with a domestic servant following in attendance.
HSÜ CHIEH   *sings*
   I held the power of the state
   in my own hands for twenty years.
   Such was my calibre as a statesman,
   my portrait was painted for posterity.
   Only on retirement did I come
   to experience the joys of country living.
   I can laugh at the nobility
   and I envy not even the immortals.

I, Hsü Chieh, have been prime minister during two reigns, and I am among the most famous men of my generation. I retired because of my advanced years, and now my estates and properties are scattered through the length and breadth of Wu. I have a thousand servants and I am rich and high in rank. What else is there to wish for? A month ago I read in the *Peking Gazette* that Hai Kang-feng had been transferred to the governorship of Kiangnan. I have not seen him for many years, but if he comes here I know he will certainly do some outstanding things.
   sings
   I am glad that my old friend brings
   his banners to govern this place.
   A man of integrity, the older he grows,
   the more resolute he becomes.
   We shall renew our old association,
   discuss poetry and literature,
   be an inspiration for youth.
   He will rule long
   and with great benevolence towards the masses.

36

Oh-oh, hold on. I was at court for many years, but my children lived in the country, and there was inevitably always some affair arising from their insulting and ridiculing of the peasants. This man Kang-feng is extremely old fashioned. What shall we do if he should dig any of this up? *contemplates* I know, I had definitely better give my children some further instruction on these matters and control them rigorously. I cannot let them stir up a lot of trouble needlessly. Even if he starts trying to dig things up, as long as there is nothing concrete for him to get his hands on, we can meet the situation satisfactorily. Really, I am very happy in one way, and yet quite apprehensive at the same time.

Enter a domestic servant.

SERVANT   I beg to inform the Grand Tutor that the Honourable Censor has come to pay his respects.

HSÜ CHIEH   Ask him in quickly, and sound the drums of welcome.

Sound of drums and music. Enter Hai Jui with Hai P'eng following.

HAI JUI   Grand Tutor.

HSÜ CHIEH   Kang-feng.

HAI JUI   Since I have taken up this post, many public affairs and responsibilities have kept me occupied, and only today have I come to pay my respects. Please forgive me.

HSÜ CHIEH   What is Kang-feng talking about? The emperor has especially dispatched you to come and govern this place and we are all grateful for this blessing. I am old and my strength has declined, so I have not gone to great lengths to welcome you. I hope you will excuse me.

They bow and then sit down.

HAI JUI   I have not seen you for many years. You have become more robust and perky than ever.

HSÜ CHIEH   Thank you, thank you, but I am old and of no use whatsoever. But my teeth are still good and I can still eat meat. Kang-feng, I presume that your honourable family has accompanied you to this post?

HAI JUI   My mother's age is very advanced, but she is also still very robust. My wife has come with me to look after her.

HSÜ CHIEH   Good, good. Another day, I shall send my daughters-in-law to call on them.

37

HAI JUI   You are too kind.

HSÜ CHIEH   Kang-feng, I am honoured by your visit today, but what is it you
             wish to speak to me about?

HAI JUI   I have come to pay my respects to the Grand Tutor. But the second
           reason for my coming is that I want to ask your advice.

HSÜ CHIEH   If I know anything that can help you, I shall of course be entirely
             sincere with you and tell you everything.

HAI JUI   The Grand Tutor was an important statesman at court and you are an
           elder in this place. You will certainly have a profound understanding
           of the merits and demerits of politics in Wuchung.[30] This is the first
           time I have ever been here. I have hopes that you will condescend to
           give me some instructions concerning what the first priorities should
           be in relation to government.

HSÜ CHIEH   Ha ha, Kang-feng, you are too modest, but since you want me to
             speak, I shall not try to beat around the bush. I shall be perfectly
             direct with my old friend.
             sings
             The wicked people in the area of Wu
             are characteristically vicious and stupid
             and so frivolous about litigation
             that pending cases are piled high as a mountain.
             To rule without coercion or petty regulations
             requires great courage.
             Uphold the law and use it to preserve
             peace in this time of instability.

HAI JUI   Thank you for your instructions. If the wicked people sue frivolously,
           I shall of course uphold the law and keep peace. And if the gentry
           break the law and oppress good people?

HSÜ CHIEH   Kang-feng, you have been absolutely upright and straightforward all
             your life. Even to the late emperor, your words were entirely direct
             when you admonished him. You will leave a fragrant name in history.
             I expect you will be even more direct with the gentry here.
             sings
             The great law of the Imperial Court
             is promulgated throughout the land.

Princes and common people
must all receive the same treatment.
Wolves barring the way must be scattered;
do not put aside your precious sword.[31]

HAI JUI　Many thanks for your advice. Ah, Grand Tutor!
sings
I recall years ago at the emperor's court,
anxiety made me lose sleep and forget to eat.
I had the courage to face the late emperor
and admonish him to rectify
bad political practices.
Now I shall dwell in the countryside
as the universal hope of the peasants here.
I shall set an example for the youth
by strict adherence to the law
and by a long and peaceful rule.

There is still one thing I wish to ask you about.

HSÜ CHIEH　Please do.

HAI JUI　Hung A-lan, a peasant woman of Hua-t'ing County, has launched a lawsuit accusing someone in your household of seizing people's fields, kidnapping a girl, and viciously beating an innocent man. How should I handle it?

HSÜ CHIEH　*pales*　What! If such a thing has happened, who is it she has accused?

HAI JUI　Hsü Ying.

HSÜ CHIEH　He is my third son. Kang-feng, you remember what kind of a man I am; you have a profound knowledge of me. These lands and estates of mine were all purchased with cash. How can anyone talk about them being seized? My son Hsü Ying is a law-abiding man. Kidnapping and beating people? He certainly would not go so far as to commit foolish crimes like that. I have just told you how these wicked people in Wu characteristically make false accusations. Kang-feng, you must pay absolutely no attention to their falsehoods.

HAI JUI　There is absolutely no truth to this affair?

HSÜ CHIEH　There is absolutely nothing to it.

39

HAI JUI   What if this affair were true?

HSÜ CHIEH   What if it were true? There is not one chance in ten thousand that it is true.

HAI JUI   What if the one chance in ten thousand occurred and the evidence was really factual?

HSÜ CHIEH   If there were proof, you should do as you see fit and handle it according to law.

HAI JUI   Good! Good! According to law, then. Well said. That being the case, I shall take my leave of you.

HSÜ CHIEH   Good day.

HAI JUI   Good day.

Drums and music. Hsü Chieh bows and Hai Jui exits.

HSÜ CHIEH   Ai ya! This affair which Kang-feng was just talking about! If one thing leads to another, this is really going to be terrible. Let me call Hsü Ying in here and I shall find out the facts of this thing. Servant, summon the Third Master to come in here.

SERVANT   Calling Third Master!

Enter Hsü Ying.

HSÜ YING   Allow me to pay my respects, father. What is it that has prompted you to call me?

HSÜ CHIEH   Someone has accused you of kidnapping and beating people. Can there be anything to this?

HSÜ YING   Why, damn! Yes, it is true, but the case has already been settled.

HSÜ CHIEH   Where was it settled?

HSÜ YING   In the Hua-t'ing County Court.

HSÜ CHIEH   How was it settled?

HSÜ YING   The District Magistrate told me to say that on that day I was studying at the home of a *hsiu-ts'ai* in this city and never left the city. Then he had the old man who had laid the charge beaten to death publicly. He settled the case by getting rid of the plaintiff.

40

HSÜ CHIEH *pales* Ai ya! He beat the man to death! He beat the man to death! You said you never went outside the city. Who did you have for a witness?

HSÜ YING Hsü Fu was a witness.

HSÜ CHIEH Do you mean the Hsü Fu of my household? *asks Hsü Fu* Were you the witness?

HSÜ FU Grand Tutor, it was no one else but your bond slave.

HSÜ CHIEH That is no good. That will not do at all. How can a family slave be a witness? *to Hsü Ying* You! This case is now going to be reported at the governor's yamen. You fool! How do you think you are going to handle it this time?

HSÜ YING Father, what is the problem about this? It cannot come to more than our having to spend some more money again. With the people they have for officials these days, I cannot imagine that there could be one who does not love money.

HSÜ CHIEH Oh, you fool! Do you know who the governor is?

HSÜ YING Does it matter who he is? Whoever he is, he cannot be more than a governor.

HSÜ CHIEH Bah! Idiot! You have rushed headlong into a calamity. This governor cannot be compared to other men. He happens to be Hai Jui, the one honest official of these times. He is honest, upright, and absolutely incorruptible. He is resolute and selfless and if he judges this case according to law, you simply need not think about living any longer.

HSÜ YING *alarmed* My God! Hai Jui! Father, what can be done about this?

HSÜ CHIEH What can be done about this? What can be done about this, indeed?

HSÜ YING Father, I have done something wrong. We must think of a way out.

HSÜ CHIEH Bah! There is no alternative to be considered. Good God! First, he beats someone half to death[32] and then he gets his bond slave to testify for him. What can one do about a thing like this? ... I have it! A virtuous man has ways of handling things. Hsü Ying, come close to me so that I may whisper in your ear.

41

HSÜ YING   Yes. *His father whispers in his ear and Hsü Ying looks pleased.*

HSÜ CHIEH   My son, I order that from now on no one in this family is to go needlessly provoking trouble and committing crimes.

HSÜ YING   Yes, father.

HSÜ CHIEH   I mean it! This cannot go on any longer.

HSÜ YING   I understand, father. I shall leave now. *exits*

HSÜ CHIEH   Ai yai yai! This charge of kidnapping and beating is indeed legitimate. When Hai Jui and I were talking just now, I was not careful. I said too much. If Kang-feng takes a firm stand on the law, there is no doubt that he will be difficult to deal with. Wait! There is another side to it. I did a kindness for him once in the past. A virtuous man repays a kindness with kindness. I would calculate that he would not turn on me now. I think my son's life may still be saved. Anyway, I cannot think of anything more than this. If it is the wrong move then it is the wrong move, but the only thing I can do is to try to handle it this way. We shall see how he handles things and cross our bridges when we come to them. In a word:

I do not worry about national affairs, but family affairs,
And I would serve as a slave for the benefit of my children.

SCENE 5 A mother's counsel

Time   Three days later.
Place   An inner court in the Soochow Governor's yamen.
Characters   HAI JUI
             HAI P'ENG
             HSIEH SHIH
             WANG SHIH

Enter Hsieh Shih and Wang Shih with a slave girl following in attendance.

HSIEH SHIH *sings*
As my son prepares
to reconvene the court
and look into this case,
so diligent is he,
loyal and devoted,
that he forgets to sleep,
ignores his food.

WANG SHIH *sings*
He will eradicate
the greedy officials
and their rapacious underlings.
Young and old will all
taste happiness together.

HSIEH SHIH My daughter-in-law! These last few days Hai P'eng has been coming to me saying that in every street and alley there is a babble of discussion. They say that the eyes of heaven have been opened. They say there really are some standards of justice and that there is a living Buddha for every family. Some say that since he has taken up his post, the dikes have been maintained and the people have been saved from the calamity of floods; they say that Hai Lung Wang[33] has come to earth. The Wusung River also floods after extended rains and he has already begun dredging operations on it. Moreover he has personally gone to the river to superintend the labour. The refugees have all gone joyously to join in the work. Besides this, he has surveyed the land and implemented the equitable "single whip policy." When she hears words like those, his old mother feels very happy. Having a son like this makes an old woman like me feel that all her efforts in bringing him up have been well worth while.

43

sings
I think of bringing up this fatherless child
and the sadness in the black of the night:
taught the *Book of Odes* and the *Book of History*,
trained to be filial,
disdaining anything improper.
We hired a strict and stern tutor
to make him study diligently;
he placed first in the local examination.
He became a magistrate,
eliminated cruel abuses of the people,
restored the basic rules of society.
Nowadays, as the Governor of Kiangnan,
he occupies a very high position.
His responsibility is very great
and the people all look up to him
in hope that he will help them
in their tribulations.

WANG SHIH   Oh, mother!
sings
I have followed my husband through ten years
of hardship in official life.
As an official, he has been
uncompromisingly upright
loyal, and brave enough
to peel the scales off a dragon.
Imprisoned in the imperial dungeon,
flogged in the audience chamber,
your son has nearly lost his life.
With his upright character
he is difficult to dissuade,
but still I hope that you might counsel him
to be more moderate.

HSIEH SHIH   Daughter-in-law, your husband is an honest and conscientious official
and he has a wide reputation for being resolutely incorruptible. He was
dismissed from office without warning and imprisoned, but he is still
the same as he always was. What he says is exactly what he means and
a hundred trials will not wear him down. This is precisely what is so
good about him. It would be best if you stopped worrying so much
about him.

44

WANG SHIH   You are right.

Enter Hai Jui, dressed in ordinary clothes, with Hai P'eng following.

HAI JUI   *sings*
The gentry and the evil officials
are feeding on the fat of the people.
The resentment of the people
bubbles and boils;
their hatred will be hard to overcome.
When troops prepare for battle,
wanting to shoot men,
they first shoot the horses
out from under them.
The various affairs of state in Kiangnan
require most careful consideration.

WANG SHIH   My Lord.

HAI JUI   Greetings, my wife. I pay my respects, mother.

HSIEH SHIH   I am glad to see you. Sit down beside me.

HAI JUI   Thank you, I shall. Ah!

HSIEH SHIH   My son, since you have come here to this post you do not think of food or drink and you have not had a peaceful sleep for many days. You should work hard as an official, but at the same time you should not overdo it and wear yourself out.

HAI JUI   Many thanks for your advice, mother. I shall take heed. Only ...

HSIEH SHIH   Only what?

HAI JUI   Ah!

HSIEH SHIH   Why does my son heave such a long sigh?

HAI JUI   There is so much that you do not know about mother. Since I have come to this position, the common people have flocked to accuse Grand Tutor Hsü of seizing their fields, allowing his son to act wickedly, oppressing the little people, and shielding the gentry. It does seem that he is concerned with wealth rather than virtue. His third son, Hsü Ying, usurped the property of the Chao family, kidnapped an orphan girl[34] in the Chao family, hounded the only Chao

45

son until he died of chagrin. And on top of all this, he bribed a corrupt official to beat to death an injured member of the Chao family. Many years ago, the Grand Tutor still had a good reputation at the court and he saved my life. But the way he seems now! Oh, this man!
sings
Although he's masked as a moralist,
discussing propriety and duty,
evil lurks within him.
His son inflicts injuries on the common people,
amasses property and wealth.
Lending money at high rates, seizing land,
they are truly shysters.
His virtues are false and his vices are real;
of that there is no doubt.

HSIEH SHIH   My son, it is not easy to know the nature of men. There is no use crying over spilt milk.[35] He was kind to you, but nevertheless he has come to hate the common people. Do you hold with private favours? What about your duty to apply the law of the country? Oh, my son!
sings
Fifty years you have studied
the classic writings of Confucius and Mencius.
Han Dynasty people buried cart-wheels[36]
and wiped out the evil classes of people.
In this dynasty, Prefect K'uang
reversed unjust prison sentences.
With ancient and contemporary men as examples,
why should you hesitate?

HAI JUI   Those are my sentiments exactly. Very well, mother! Tomorrow I shall reopen the court. The first thing I shall do is to deal with Hsü Ying according to law. Second, I shall make the Hsü family give back all the property which they have taken forcefully from the people. Third, I shall issue a proclamation saying that any gentry who have unlawfully seized land from the people must return it to the original owners, under penalty of law. But I particularly wanted to hear your advice, mother.

HAI P'ENG   My Lord, excuse your old servant for speaking frankly.
sings
Throughout the entire country,
those in official positions

46

mistreat the common people.
Though they suffer pain and distress,
nowhere can they seek redress.
Grand Tutor Hsü has great influence
and is of a vicious and sinister mind.
Do not do anything hasty
that might bring a hornet's nest down on your head.

HAI JUI   What you say is not correct. It certainly will not do for me to be
afraid of the Hsü family, just because it has great influence!
sings
What is it in your experience
that accounts for this kind of talk?
Though I, Hai Jui, have endured many hardships,
yet my will remains undiminished.
Getting rid of the tyrants
and assuaging the people's anger
requires a man's will.
However great his power,
I will deal with him.

WANG SHIH   My husband, there is still merit in Hai P'eng's words, and I still hope
you will think them over carefully.
sings
These several years you have received
the emperor's favour, and your rank
has risen steadily. Protector of this region
and overseer of its great affairs,
you have formed flawless plans.
But if you kill Hsü Ying,
uphold the country's law,
ignore your own concerns,
they will say you have forgotten
old obligations, and cast aside
favours that were done you.
On top of that, think of his power.
His connections are both local and at court;
his power is immense.
This is no small matter:
consider it most carefully.
Do not let this result in the sorrow
and trouble of his wrathful retribution.

47

HAI JUI My wife, what are you talking about? When that Hsü Chieh allows his son to act wickedly, if I, Hai Jui, paid attention to personal obligations and forgot the law of the country, how could I face my beloved mother, or the emperor, or the people?
sings
When the son of Grand Tutor Hsü
is kidnapping girls and committing murder,
and the people lose their property
and are taxed into poverty,
what is the use of studying great books
if I consider private obligations
and forget the law?
To protect the borders
and comfort the common people,
one must govern very fairly.

HSIEH SHIH My son, my daughter-in-law, Hai P'eng! If one is to heed the sacred books and do virtuous deeds, the law of the country must be upheld and the people delivered from their hardships. My son must be concerned only with the impartial observance and implementation of the law. He should think only of answering to the emperor on the one hand, and maintaining the peace of the people on the other.
sings
I am glad my son applies himself
to the people's problems,
putting first the upholding of the law.
To wipe out the tyrants and support the small and weak
is to be very virtuous.
Grand Tutor Hsü is a man of wide experience.
His calculations have far-reaching consequence.
But his son has flouted the country's law
and surely must be punished.
Your mother and wife support you in the family
and are unconcerned with high position.
With simple, homely food
and plain clothes and shoes,
we can be happier than the gods.
Even if it means that some of these people
will undermine you, cause your downfall,
you can return to Ch'iung-chow and enjoy
the sight of green water and blue mountains.

48

HAI JUI Many thanks for your advice, mother. My wife, mother has become weary, how about taking her into the court for a little rest?

Exit Wang Shih, supporting Hsieh Shih.

HAI JUI Hai P'eng, go and issue the order for the court to resume sessions tomorrow. Summon everyone connected with the case of Hung A-lan to appear. The officials of the two prefectures of Soochow and Sungkiang will sit in judgment on the case. There must be no mistake about this.

HAI P'ENG Very well. *exits*

HAI JUI In a word:

I must apply the laws of the emperor,
and kill these greedy, corrupt officials. *exits*

SCENE 6   The lawsuit is continued

Time   The next day.
Place   The Great Court in the Soochow Governor's yamen.
Characters   HAI JUI.
The officials of Soochow and Sungkiang prefectures.
HUNG A-LAN and a large group of peasants.
HSÜ YING, accompanied by HSÜ FU (wearing the cap and gown of a *hsiu-ts'ai*).
The director of the Hua-t'ing District Academy.
Standard-bearers, officers, soldiers, and many yamen runners.

Enter the officials of Soochow and Sungkiang prefectures.

CHENG YÜ   *recites*
Every day I wait before the yamen gate for an audience.

LI P'ING-TU   It makes me feel very worried inside and ill at ease,

HSIAO YEN   Why do they not come and summon us?

WANG MING-YU   Night and day, I feel as if I am sitting on pins and needles.

HSIAO YEN   Gentlemen, Censor Hai came to this position wearing everyday apparel, and so we did not receive him. Now he shuts his doors up tight and never comes out and for the most part never receives any military or civilian officials. All he does every day is go to the river to superintend labour. And he summons the lower classes and the poor, the peasants, workers, and merchants to him so that he can ask them questions. Does no one know the reason for this?

CHENG YÜ   It was his own doing that we did not meet him and welcome him, since he entered the city wearing ordinary clothes. I do not think this would cause him to blame us for anything. It is just that since taking office he has not resumed public business or the sittings of the court. Everything is in a state of limbo, waiting for him to do something. When he never comes forward to take up his responsibilities, it is certain to make people anxious.

LI P'ING-TU   It certainly is strange! First he orders us to come here and wait for an audience, and then, several days later, he still has not summoned us. Doesn't anyone know what the purpose of this is?

50

WANG MING-YU Every day we have come here to wait before the yamen gate for an audience, yet there still is not a sign of life from in there. It really does make a person anxious.

Enter a standard-bearer.

STANDARD-
BEARER His Lordship has ordered the gate to be opened. Court is now in session.

Exit the group of officials. Enter officers, soldiers, and yamen runners, to the sound of drums and music. Enter Hai Jui, wearing a red robe and silk cap.

HAI JUI *recites*
Restore the rule of law, in the name of the people;
injustice must be redressed.
The people have suffered cruel treatment
and can bear no more.
The gentry have presumed to conduct themselves
in an evil and vicious fashion.
Slaying the scaly dragon and shooting the tiger
are affairs for a man.
Why should one deserve a plaque for virtuous government
simply for doing his duty?

I, the Ying T'ien Governor, Hai Jui, since taking office, have been investigating the unreasonable and unlawful conduct of the rich gentry class. Avaricious and corrupt officials have been oppressing the people. In cases where there is factual evidence against the people concerned, we shall expend our full effort in eliminating the evildoers. The state has punishments to deal with them. Today, I am reopening the court. I am determined to set up a system of laws which will relieve the suffering of the people. Attendants, call all the officials to come in here before me.

STANDARD-
BEARER The officials of Soochow and Sungkiang prefectures are to come in before the governor.

Enter all the officials, each announced as he presents himself.

ALL THE
OFFICIALS The officials of the two prefectures of Soochow and Sungkiang report to the Honourable Censor. When Your Lordship came here to fill this office, we missed the opportunity to welcome you. We beseech your forgiveness.

HAI JUI Thank you very much for coming to welcome me. But the reason

51

you did not meet me was that I came to take up my duties wearing ordinary clothes and without using a dispatch horse, so what is there to forgive? Moreover, we have met before, so why is any further formality necessary?

LI P'ING-TU   May I ask His Lordship the Censor where it was that we met previously?

HAI JUI   It was right in front of the Official Welcoming Pavilion. Please lift your eyes and let us recognize one another.

All the officials look up, startled. Li P'ing-tu becomes alarmed and flustered; he feels like crawling into a hole.

HAI JUI   There is a matter I wish to talk over with you. Please be seated.

ALL THE
OFFICIALS   Thank you.

CHENG YÜ   My Lord Censor, I summon all my courage in order that I might dare to ask you if you have fixed a date to resume business and allow complaints to be heard?

HAI JUI   Why is it necessary to select a date? I am resuming business right today and I shall allow complaints to be heard. Standard-bearer, proclaim the resumption of official business and the opening of the court for complaints.

STANDARD-
BEARER   Your command is received.

The standard-bearer takes the seal and stamps the tablet proclaiming the opening of court. A soldier picks up the tablet and goes off.

HAI JUI   Gentlemen.

ALL THE
OFFICIALS   Your Lordship, the Great Censor.

HAI JUI   How do you conduct yourselves as officials?

ALL THE
OFFICIALS   We are absolutely honest and meticulously careful officials. We manage things in the interest of the Imperial Court, and we mitigate the misery of the common people.

HAI JUI   Is that a fact? You really manage things in the interest of the Imperial Court, and mitigate the misery of the common people?

52

ALL THE OFFICIALS Absolutely.

HAI JUI Ha ha! Well, since you are all absolutely honest officials, there is a case about which I would like to question all you gentlemen together and hear your judgments. Where is the Hua-t'ing District Magistrate?

WANG MING-YU I am here.

HAI JUI I would like to ask you how you disposed of the case of Hung A-lan?

WANG MING-YU This case ... this case ... I handled it with justice. It is already settled.

HAI JUI What was your way of settling it with justice?

WANG MING-YU Hung A-lan charged that on the day of the Ch'ing-ming Festival, Hsü Ying had kidnapped her daughter and beaten her father-in-law, causing him serious injury. I summoned the accused and made an inquiry. On that day of the Ch'ing-ming Festival, Hsü Ying was at Scholar Chang's house, studying. Moreover, he never went outside the city. It was obvious that the vicious person was making a false accusation, so I drove her out of the court. We cannot tolerate such cases as these.

HAI JUI If Hsü Ying never went outside the city on the day of the Ch'ing-ming Festival, who can testify to that effect?

WANG MING-YU The Hsü family's head servant accompanied him in attendance and he testified in court.

HAI JUI Oh! There was a witness. The Hsü family's bond slave was a witness! Good! The next thing I would like to ask you about is the manner in which Chao Yü-shan died.

WANG MING-YU Why, why ... it happened while I was giving him a few very light strokes of the cane. Who could know that because he was so old, he would just go suddenly – like that?

HAI JUI Ha ha! Ha ha! How well you put it: he just went suddenly. It is a good thing that you handled everything according to justice. Standard-bearer, summon Hung A-lan and the witnesses concerned to come into court.

The standard-bearer calls out the summons. Enter Hung A-lan, all the peasants, Hsü Ying, and Hsü Fu.

53

HUNG A-LAN *wailing bitterly* Your Worship! Redress the wrongs which have been done me!

HAI JUI There is no need for you to lament in this way. Just speak the truth.

HUNG A-LAN Oh, Your Worship!
sings
Having suffered injustice, full of bitterness,
I have harboured this grievance until now.
My husband, his land seized by evil tyrants,
was so vexed he died of chagrin.
During the Ch'ing-ming Festival they stole my beautiful daughter,
brutally beat my father-in-law.
Why did Magistrate Wang beat the injured party to death,
on perjured evidence?

HAI JUI Her land seized, her husband hounded to death, her daughter kidnapped, her father-in-law beaten to death. How pitiable, how pitiable! Disgusting, disgusting! Oh, how hateful! Hsü Ying!

HSÜ YING I am here.

HAI JUI Hung A-lan has accused you of usurping land, of kidnapping, and of beating people. Can these things be true?

HSÜ YING I am a junior member of the family of a statesman, a very scholarly family. How could I stoop to such a lawless act? Moreover, on that particular day of the Ch'ing-ming Festival, I actually never went outside the city. I have Scholar Chang of this city as a witness. This case has already been fairly concluded by His Worship, Hua-t'ing District Magistrate Wang. So I hope His Honour the Great Censor will not simply listen to the version given by these wicked people, but will have some regard for my father's position and settle this case justly.

HAI JUI Since there is a witness, it should be easy to settle this case.

HSÜ YING I shall give my evidence through an intermediary and, according to the universal principle, if the evidence is false, I am willing to undergo the appropriate punishment.

HAI JUI It is wonderful of you to say that you are willing to undergo punishment if your evidence is false. Scholar Chang.

HSÜ FU   I am here.

HAI JUI   You must tell the truth. On that day of the Ch'ing-ming Festival, was Hsü Ying really at your house studying?

HSÜ FU   That is the absolute truth. On that day, Third Master Hsü was not only studying, but writing an essay.

HAI JUI   What essay was he writing?

HSÜ FU   *agape with astonishment*   He wrote the "Thousand Character Essay." No, that is not correct. What he wrote was the "Hundred Family Surnames." [37]

Hsü Ying pales, stamps his foot.

HAI JUI   *banging the table*   The nerve of you, you blackguard. What should the punishment be for impersonating a *hsiu-ts'ai*?

HSÜ FU   I would not dare to do such a thing. My cap is legitimate; [38] I am not an impostor.

HAI JUI   It is legitimate; you are not an impostor. Well, that is good. I would like to ask you, what year did you enter the academy?

HSÜ FU   Why, why ...

HSÜ YING   If I may inform the Honourable Governor, I can testify that he really is a *hsiu-ts'ai* from the District Academy.

HAI JUI   Silence. Is the Director of the Hua-t'ing Academy here?
ACADEMY
DIRECTOR   I am here.

HAI JUI   Is he a graduate of your school?
ACADEMY
DIRECTOR   I have never seen him before. This man is certainly not from our school.

Hsü Ying trembles; Hsü Fu kneels on the ground.

HAI JUI   So! The great gall of you, you villain! To impersonate *literati* and give false evidence in order to bring undeserved suffering on good people! Attendants, take him out and flog him to death.

55

HSÜ FU *kowtows* Save my life, Your Worship. I shall testify according to the real facts.

HAI JUI If you tell the real facts, I shall spare your life. Who are you?

HSÜ FU I am Hsü Fu, Third Master Hsü's servant.

HAI JUI Since you are a servant, why did you impersonate a *hsiu-ts'ai*?

HSÜ FU I deserve to die but I was ordered to impersonate him. I did not do it voluntarily.

HAI JUI Impertinent bond slave, I shall ask you once more. Where *did* Hsü Ying go on the day of the Ch'ing-ming Festival?

HSÜ FU He went to the graveyard on Heng Yün Mountain for an outing.

HAI JUI Was Chao Hsiao-lan kidnapped by Hsü Ying, and where is she now?

HSÜ FU I kidnapped her on the orders of the Young Master and we gave her a fearful beating when she would not submit to him. At present, she is still locked up in his house.

HAI JUI Why did you also beat Chao Yü-shan?

HSÜ FU When we were carrying out the kidnapping, Chao Yü-shan blocked our way. So the Young Master ordered us to beat him.

HAI JUI How serious were his injuries?

HSÜ FU He had scars all over his body. His injuries were very grave.

HAI JUI The Hua-t'ing Magistrate examined the injuries, so how was it that he said there weren't any?

HSÜ FU On the orders of the Young Master, I bought off the prefect, the magistrate, and the coroner. The coroner accepted our bribe and he therefore said that there were no injuries.

Li P'ing-tu and Wang Ming-yu arise, trembling.

HAI JUI How much did you bribe them? Who witnessed it? Speak the truth.

56

HSÜ FU   Three hundred taels of gold for the prefect, and two hundred taels of gold for the magistrate.

Wang Ming-yu, Li P'ing-tu, and Hsü Ying kneel down, trembling.

HAI JUI   Did you yourself hand it over?

HSÜ FU   It was handed over by me personally.

HAI JUI   What were the circumstances of Chao Yü-shan's death?

HSÜ FU   He was beaten to death by the Hua-t'ing District Magistrate. This is how the lawsuit was won.

HAI JUI   Did you see this with your own eyes?

HSÜ FU   With my own eyes.

Wang Ming-yu, Li P'ing-tu, and Hsü Ying kowtow, confessing their crimes and begging for mercy.

HAI JUI   *sings*
These avaricious and corrupt officials
are entirely without conscience.
It is in vain that they dress
in the official robes of the court.
Today I shall certainly quell
the resentment of the people.
The law will be as firm
and solid as a mountain, showing no mercy.

This is the sentence: Hsü Ying abducted a girl, savagely beat a common man, bribed the prefect, and gave false evidence which led to the killing of another man. In accordance with the law, he will be strangled. As for his family property, aside from what is returned to his victims, the rest will be confiscated by the state. Chao Hsiao-lan is to be reunited with Hung A-lan. Wang Ming-yu received bribes, administered the law crookedly, and killed the plaintiff by beating. According to law, he will be beheaded. Li P'ing-tu, nicknamed Li Po-p'i, you have been greedy, corrupt, and dishonest. You are to be stripped of your rank and imprisoned at the pleasure of the Imperial Court. Hsü Fu has impersonated a *hsiu-ts'ai*, given bribes, and committed perjury. Considering that he did not do this voluntarily and that he has, moreover, now testified according to the law, he shall receive one hundred strokes of the cane and banishment for three

57

years. The coroner has received bribes and committed perjury. He will be stripped of his duties, and according to law he will receive one hundred strokes of the cane and banishment for two years. Gentlemen, are the sentences fair?

CHENG YÜ The Great Censor has removed the abuses of the people. I support you.

HSÜ YING *kowtows* Great and Honourable Censor, please have regard for my father's face and save my life.

HAI JUI Silence. When a prince violates the law, the punishment is the same as for an ordinary man. Take him away.

The soldiers bind Wang Ming-yu, Li P'ing-tu, Hsü Ying, and Hsü Fu, and all exit.

HAI JUI Hung A-lan, do you have anything more to say?

HUNG A-LAN Your Worship has erased the hatred among the people. Long life to you, noble sir. *kowtows*

HAI JUI Elders,[39] the day before yesterday we had a chat. Many thanks for your counsel. This case is now closed; is there anything you would like to say?

FIRST PEASANT Your Worship's judgment is extremely fair! It is only that our lands were stolen by the Hsüs and other gentry families. The property is gone but the taxes remain, so that the lives of the people are full of hardship. We hope that Your Worship can also do something about this for us.

SECOND PEASANT
THIRD PEASANT Please act in our interest, Your Worship.

HAI JUI Standard-bearer, I want you to issue this order for me and publish notices of it. Within the time limit of ten days, every gentry family which has seized land from the people will return all of it. I shall not accept any delay. If they disobey, they will be punished according to law.

STANDARD-BEARER Your command is received.

ALL THE *kowtowing* Your Worship has acted for the people. From now on
PEASANTS there will be happy days in store for the poor people of Kiangnan!
We are much obliged to you for your kindness. We shall return home
and paint a portrait of Your Worship, which we shall honour morning
and evening!
all sing
These days we shall look up to Heaven above,
We shall plough and sow diligently,
restoring orchards and gardens.
While we have land, what worry have we
for clothes and food?
A promising future lies before our eyes.

Our humble thanks, Your Worship!

HAI JUI There is no need to go on like this. You had better leave now.

Exit Hung A-lan and all the peasants, still expressing their gratitude.

CHENG YÜ
HSIAO YEN We shall take our leave now.

HAI JUI Not so fast. Wu District Magistrate.

HSIAO YEN Yes.

HAI JUI You are greedy, corrupt, and extravagant. You have a bad reputation
as an official. Do you acknowledge these faults?

HSIAO YEN I acknowledge them.

HAI JUI You are cashiered and sent home. Standard-bearer, remove his silk
cap.

Standard-bearer removes Hsiao Yen's silk cap. Exit Hsiao Yen.

HAI JUI Prefect of Soochow.

CHENG YÜ Yes.

HAI JUI You are to instruct all the officials to put their minds at ease and resume their duties. There is no need to harbour any uneasiness.

CHENG YÜ Very well. I shall go now.

Exit Cheng Yü.

59

HAI JUI   Ha ha, for ten days now I have had to occupy myself solely with the handling of this case. The irrigation system on the Wusung River is right in the middle of repairs and the Pai Mao River needs dredging. The reforms of the "single whip policy" must be extended to the people. I shall do all of these things one by one and the common people will breathe a little easier. In a word:

I shall expend every effort
to eliminate greed and corruption,
and revitalize government.
I intend to act in the interests
of the common people. *exits*

Exit the standard-bearer and soldiers, carrying a placard, beating a gong, and reading out the proclamation.

STANDARD-
BEARER   All gentry and commoners, hear this: Censor Hai of the Imperial Court of Censors, Governor of Ying T'ien and the Ten Prefectures, in relation to the matter of returning land, proclaims for all to know: Evil gentry tyrants have usurped land belonging to the people. The innocent people, having lost their property, are in a state of helpless dependence and hardship. According to the law of the country, the land is to be given back. Whoever dares to disobey will be inviting punishment.

All the people listen quietly and then go off, dancing happily to the sound of drums. Exit standard-bearer and soldiers.

60

SCENE 7   Asking a favour

Time   Three days later.
Place   The yamen of the Soochow Governor.
Characters   HAI JUI and HAI P'ENG.
   HSÜ CHIEH and a domestic servant from the Hsü household.

*Enter Hsü Chieh, dressed in ordinary clothes and riding on a sedan
chair, with his domestic servant following in attendance.*

HSÜ CHIEH   *sings*
   I regret that I left the Imperial Court
   and lost the emperor's favour.
   I have no alternative now
   but to protect my estate for my children;
   otherwise all my efforts will come to nought.
   Oh, how bitter, to have an unfilial son
   who acts so rashly and violates criminal law.
   In my old age, to have to watch my grandson,
   son, and daughter weeping in their grief,
   how can my heart endure it?
   I shall forget my face and go
   to beg my old friend to overlook the law
   and act according to his feelings.

   Ah! Things have come to such a state that I can no longer have any
   regard for face. As long as I can succeed in my plea that my son
   should not die, we need not bother to quibble about anything else.
   Ah!
   continues song
   But I hope that Censor Hai
   will remember our old friendship
   and lend a helping hand to save his life.
   If I can get this,
   though I gnash my teeth to the roots,
   I shall forsake my property,
   and whether they fine me lightly or heavily,
   I shall comply.

   We have arrived at the Governor's yamen. Servant, go forward and
   announce us.

SERVANT   Who is on the gate?

61

YAMEN SENTRY What is it?

SERVANT Grand Tutor Hsü pays a return visit to Censor Hai.

YAMEN SENTRY Wait here while I report it. Excuse me, Your Worship, Grand Tutor Hsü has come to pay respects.

Enter Hai Jui

HAI JUI Grand Tutor Hsü has come to return my call. Indeed, so he has. Come in, please.

HSÜ CHIEH Kang-feng, the day before yesterday[40] you came to see me. Today, I have come especially to return your visit.

HAI JUI I am greatly honoured. Please be seated.

HSÜ CHIEH Thank you.

HAI JUI Am I correct in judging from the Grand Tutor's appearance that there is something troubling you?

HSÜ CHIEH You certainly are correct. Oh, Kang-feng!
sings
In my old age and feeble infirmity,
Hsü Ying, the violator of the law, is my son.
I beg you to consider me and cover up his crimes,
and give him a light sentence to comfort me.

HAI JUI Grand Tutor!
sings
Stealing land, abducting girls is a heavy crime.
Open bribery, killing poor people:
you have no care whatever for the law.
How can the law be so elastic
as to be changed at will?

HSÜ CHIEH Lord Hai, every other son that I have raised has already died. Of all my children, there is only this one son left. I still have the hope that you will remember my old age and show some leniency.
sings
In my old age, I love my son
and he looks after me from dawn to dusk.
The love of parents for their offspring is
a happiness ordained by Heaven.

62

I beg you, deign to remember me,
bestow some pity on me.
I shall be grateful for your kindness,
repay your goodness and remember it forever.

HAI JUI   Grand Tutor, you know all about the love you have for your son, but do you know anything about Hung A-lan's daughter, or her husband, or her father-in-law? And it is not only Hung A-lan. Besides her, how many orphans and widows are there? Are they all people without parents or sons and daughters?

sings

The law of the land remains as firm
and steadfast as a mountain.
The Grand Tutor once instructed me
that when the law is broken,
no matter if the offender be of noble rank or low,
both prince and pauper will be treated
with absolute equality.

HSÜ CHIEH   Oh! Oh! You are right. I did say something to that effect. But many years ago, Lord Hai was incarcerated in the Imperial Prison, and it was I who went before the emperor with entreaties for your release. Now there is a chance for you to repay the favour. I beg you to think it over once more. Oh, Lord Hai!

sings

You were punished many years ago
for violating the law of the emperor.
How can you forget that it was I
who begged for your release?
I put my head into the lion's mouth,
I interceded with the emperor.
It is only because of this that you are here
today as governor of this area.

HAI JUI   Grand Tutor, many years ago I irritated the late emperor, and it is true that it was through you I was released and saved. But I had sent in a memorial criticizing the emperor because I was loyal to my sovereign and loved my country. How could that be considered committing a crime? Hsü Ying has beaten people and transgressed the criminal law. This is an unpardonable offence and it is abundantly clear that the two things are not comparable. How can you speak about them in the same sentence?

63

sings
Hai Jui is loyal to his emperor
and has a fragrant reputation;
Hsü Ying is a ruthless offender
of the law of the land.
"Maintain a fair balance and uphold the law,"
the Grand Tutor has said.
"When eliminating evil, first one must
eliminate the wolf that blocks the way."

HSÜ CHIEH That is right! That is right! I really did say those things about maintaining a fair balance and upholding the law. And since this is the
case, I am willing to hand over a part of my estate in order to atone
for my son's crime.
sings
My son has broken the law;
I have no face left.
I shall give land to pay for his crime;
I shall pay grain for military provisions.
The law states clearly an offence
can be paid off in grain.
You can save a man's life
and simultaneously uphold the law.

HAI JUI Handing over land is another thing altogether. I have already issued a
proclamation stating that any gentry who have usurped land belonging
to the people will have to restore it to the original owners, under penalty of law. Your family has stolen two hundred thousand *mou*[41] from
the people. It will be returned to them as a matter of course under the
law.
sings
The gentry surpass even the tiger
and the wolf in treachery.
They usurp the land of the people
and then they pay no taxes.
The people in Kiangnan
lead cold and lonely lives of hardship.
Unless their stolen land's returned,
they will not long be able to go on.

HSÜ CHIEH *turns his back to the audience* Two hundred thousand *mou*! Two
hundred thousand *mou*! You want to have the land returned and
carry out the death sentence as well! You are making me furious.

64

Hai Jui, Hai Jui, you have gone absolutely mad! *faces Hai Jui* All right, Lord Hai, you had better listen to what I have to say:
sings
You are a man who conducts himself
very sternly and strictly.
You see only one side of a problem,
ignoring the major aspects,
but disaster yet awaits you.
All the gentry you have injured
will be of the same mind and purpose,
and I fear that you will not be wearing
your black silk cap much longer.

HAI JUI   Bah! Ha ha, ha ha! My black silk cap? I do not even fear death, so can you imagine how much less important it is to me whether I go on wearing a black silk cap! All right! All right! *takes off his black silk cap*
sings
Poor students for twenty years,
studying diligently as they learn
to write their essays,
talking of Confucius and Mencius,
discussing the *Book of Songs* and *Book of History*,
these people end up losing their direction
all because of you.
Should I imitate the compromisers, I
would be ashamed to face the emperor.

Grand Tutor Hsü, here is my black silk cap, here it is! Hai Jui wants not only to be an official, but to be a man, with nothing to be ashamed of. When the decree comes, I shall return home immediately.

HSÜ CHIEH   Lord Hai, you really will not take our old friendship into consideration?

HAI JUI   I administer the law of the emperor. I could not think of letting personal considerations take precedence over the public good!

HSÜ CHIEH   You cannot reduce Hsü Ying's sentence?

HAI JUI   The Grand Tutor has said that I should uphold the law and maintain balance, treating princes and paupers absolutely alike! "If there was proof of the crime," it was to be handled "according to law."

HSÜ CHIEH   There is no way that the return of the land can be avoided?

65

HAI JUI   Usurping land belonging to the people is absolutely repugnant to reason or emotion. Certainly it shall be returned!

HSÜ CHIEH   You cannot compromise even a little bit?

HAI JUI   When it comes to upholding the law, I am absolutely implacable. I cannot compromise even one iota!

HSÜ CHIEH   Very well! Very well! Hai Jui, I hope you do not have any regrets later on.

HAI JUI   I have no thought for life or death, glory or shame. I decidedly will not have any regrets.

HSÜ CHIEH   When you speak like this, does it mean that our friendship is broken off?

HAI JUI   It is finished!

HSÜ CHIEH   Ha ha! Hai Jui!
sings
You are a mad and seditious man,
fishing for praise and reputation,
You dare to do injury
to the entire gentry class collectively.
You refuse to listen to this old man's words of wisdom,
but how do you think you will end up later on?

HAI JUI   *sings*
There is no need for the Grand Tutor to say more;
Hai Jui is patriotic and loyal
to his Imperial Majesty.
Even though I lose my position
and am misunderstood,
my name will still shed fragrance
through thousands of years of history.

Goodbye.

Exit Hsü Chieh, in a rage.

HAI JUI   I had anticipated that the old man would come here and make a scene, and indeed I was right. I do not think he will be willing to just sit back and accept this. Of the various affairs of state in Kiangnan, the elimination of the tyrants, the land survey, implementation of the "single whip

66

policy," the regulation of the irrigation system, and the return of the land – these five important matters must be concluded at an early date, in order that hundreds of thousands of ordinary people will be able to live happy lives, and also in order to lessen some of the worries of the emperor. In a word:

Though I am old, my bones are proud as ever.
How could they bend to ingratiate me
with a powerful minister.

picking up the silk cap This silk cap! This silk cap! Ha ha! Ha ha!
exits

SCENE 8 The counterattack

Time   The next day.
Place   The apartments of Hsü Chieh in Hua-t'ing County.
Characters HSÜ CHIEH.
          Two close friends of the Hsü family.
          The Hsü family secretary.

Enter the two friends of the Hsü family.

FIRST FRIEND *recites*
          My heart has been in my mouth ever since
          Hai Ch'ing-t'ien suddenly came on the scene.

SECOND FRIEND We must make plans. We villains
          cannot just calmly watch our own defeat.

FIRST FRIEND Old friend, Censor Hai has issued a proclamation that the land must
          be returned. What can we do about this?

SECOND FRIEND My family also received a copy of the proclamation. From the way
          he speaks, I think he really means business. It seems there is no way
          to get out of returning it.

FIRST FRIEND How can you bear to return something which represents a whole life's
          work?

SECOND FRIEND Who can bear it?

FIRST FRIEND Where are you going?

SECOND FRIEND I am going to find our good friend Hsü.

FIRST FRIEND I'm on my way to find him too, for a discussion. His third son has
          been sentenced to death and our good friend Hsü has gone to the
          governor's place to beg Lord Hai for leniency. I shall wait until he
          returns. He will certainly have some news.

SECOND FRIEND In that case, we might as well go there together.

FIRST FRIEND We are here. Who is on the gate?

          Enter a domestic servant.

68

SERVANT Oh, it is you two. The Grand Tutor has still not come back home, but you are welcome to wait for him in the rear court.

FIRST FRIEND Then ask the secretary to come and have a chat with us.

SERVANT I shall ask the secretary.

Enter the secretary.

FIRST FRIEND The Grand Tutor still has not come home, so we are going to wait for him here for a while.

SECOND FRIEND Lord Hai has commanded that the land be returned. In every prefecture and district the gentry are extremely angry. They are all discussing it and everyone hopes that the Grand Tutor will come up with an idea.

SECRETARY According to his proclamation, what he wants returned is the land which was forcibly seized. This is something which one simply cannot argue against. It is very difficult even for the Grand Tutor.

FIRST FRIEND He has posted notices that complaints will be heard and thousands upon thousands of the vicious people are coming to make false accusations against us gentry. The lower classes are upsetting everything. What is this world coming to?

SECRETARY The common people in Kiangnan always loved litigation in the first place, but now, with him urging them on, they have gone beyond all reason.

SECOND FRIEND Secretary, do you think it would be possible to hold a re-trial in Hsü Ying's case?

SECRETARY Lord Hai and the Grand Tutor have been close friends for many years. A few days ago he even came here to call, and today the Grand Tutor is returning his visit. I think that if Lord Hai attaches any importance to their friendship, he will give him a lighter sentence; but still, there is no way of knowing.

FIRST FRIEND Of course. The Grand Tutor was prime minister during two reigns and Lord Hai has always looked on him with favour.

Enter Hsü Chieh and his domestic servant.

69

FIRST FRIEND	
SECOND FRIEND	
SECRETARY	The Grand Tutor has returned.

HSÜ CHIEH   Yes, I have returned and I am so angry I could die!

FIRST FRIEND	
SECOND FRIEND	
SECRETARY	What? Censor Hai does not even show deference to the Grand Tutor?

HSÜ CHIEH   What deference? He wants the land returned and the execution is still going to go ahead.

FIRST FRIEND
SECOND FRIEND   Ai ya! If even the Grand Tutor cannot do anything with him, we might as well give up.

HSÜ CHIEH   Do not be so quick to give up the ship. If we all discuss it thoroughly together, we may be able to come up with an idea.

FIRST FRIEND   We and all the gentry in every prefecture and county have all discussed it already. If the Grand Tutor can come up with a solution, everyone is prepared to share the expenses.

HSÜ CHIEH   We shall pull the rug out from underneath him. We must get rid of this cursed official. At present, we are enduring a temporary defeat, but when we get a new official, will the world not belong to us again?

SECOND FRIEND   Yes! Yes! I have a plan. We shall gather all the gentry together and send a memorial to the throne. We shall accuse him of inciting the wicked people, provoking the lower classes to revolt, oppressing the gentry, and ruining discipline.

HSÜ CHIEH   That is no good. When you send in a memorial to the throne, it is discussed month after month for a whole year in some outer court. Far away water is no use in putting out a nearby fire.

FIRST FRIEND   I have an idea ... we can expend a large amount of money and hire an assassin to stab him. That way we shall solve the problem at its root.

HSÜ CHIEH   That is even worse. Since he is in command of the military and has personal guards, it could not be done. In the second place, if by one chance in ten thousand the scheme should leak out, remember that to murder the greatest official of this territory is no small crime.

70

FIRST FRIEND
SECOND FRIEND   This is no good, that is no good. If that is the way you feel, we had
                better admit we are beaten.

HSÜ CHIEH   What do you mean, beaten? Let's all try to think of another idea.

SECRETARY   Grand Tutor, I have an idea.

FIRST FRIEND
SECOND FRIEND   Let's hear it quickly.

SECRETARY   Accuse him of oppressing the gentry – of course you should accuse
            him. But if you want it to be handled quickly, you must work
            through an insider. If there is someone at the palace whom the
            Grand Tutor knows well, write him a letter in your hand, send him
            an expensive gift, and get him to expedite the approval of the mem-
            orial. Then pull some strings and bribe some of your friends from
            this area who are now officials in the capital to hand in the memorial
            accusing him. With a double-barrelled attack like this, we shall hit
            him from all sides at once. As soon as he leaves here, our situation
            will be a thousand percent happier.

HSÜ CHIEH   This is an excellent plan. We shall pull the rug out from under him
            and get immediate results. However, if he is only transferred to an-
            other post, it will not satisfy my hatred of him. I shall be satisfied
            only if we can fix it so that he can never become an official again.

FIRST FRIEND
SECOND FRIEND   Indeed it is a good plan, and for our part, we ask the Grand Tutor to
                go ahead with it.

HSÜ CHIEH   *sings*
            To protect their families, many friends
            engaged in long discussions.
            Combining the ideas and strength
            of many men, we'll set the trap.
            We'll send someone to secure an insider,
            and I shall write a letter.
            Then we shall wait and see how you make out, Hai Kang-feng!

FIRST FRIEND
SECOND FRIEND   If this is what we are going to do, there should be no delay. All the
                gentry will share expenses equally, and we must send someone

71

immediately. He should start on his journey to the capital by this very evening.

HSÜ CHIEH   So it is the opinion of my friends that I should send the letter immediately. We shall need to raise three thousand taels of gold among us: two thousand taels for the eunuch in the palace, and one thousand for our colleague in the capital. We had better all discuss which of the officials in the capital would be best.

SECOND FRIEND   Tai Feng-hsiang, the *Kei Shih-chung*[42] of Chia-hsing is a relative of mine. His family has also been forced to return land, so he will certainly be willing to expend every effort on our behalf.

HSÜ CHIEH   Tai Feng-hsiang is my student. He definitely will make the effort for us. I shall ask you to go to the capital, leaving immediately on a swift horse. What ho!

SECOND FRIEND   Right. I'll have to pack my bags, so I shall leave now.

Exit First Friend, Second Friend, and Secretary.

HSÜ CHIEH   Ha ha! Ha ha!

He shall ride into the capital
and procure a courtier's services.
I shall not rest till Kang-feng's driven off.   *exits*

SCENE 9 Dismissed from office

Time A certain day five months later.
Place The Great Court in the yamen of the Soochow Governor.
Characters HAI JUI.
TAI FENG-HSIANG, fifty years old, newly appointed to the position
of Ying T'ien Governor.
HSÜ CHIEH.
HSÜ YING and WANG MING-YU.
Tai Feng-hsiang's standard-bearers, officers, soldiers and runners.

*Tai Feng-hsiang comes on wearing a silk cap and red robe, followed
by standard-bearers, officers, soldiers, runners, and a procession of
banners and parasols.*

TAI FENG-HSIANG *recites*
I have come to Kiangnan:
this is a promotion.
What difficulty will there be
in making a hundred thousand here?
The wealthy and the powerful
I must not punish – just ignore them.
I'll simply go along my way,
not rock the boat;
all will be peaceful.

I am Tai Feng-hsiang, the newly appointed Ying T'ien Governor.
Yesterday, a letter came from the Grand Tutor, asking me to hurry
there. That is why I am galloping there in great haste.

Exit Tai Feng-hsiang and his party.
Enter Hsü Chieh.

HSÜ CHIEH *recites*
I gallop on my way
to welcome the new governor,
doing all I can to save my son's life.
The clerk in the criminal department
of the governor's yamen has told me
the imperial decree from the fall assizes
will arrive within a day or so.
Already the new governor, Tai Feng-hsiang,
has started his journey here to save my son.
I am galloping to welcome the newly appointed governor
and that is why I am in this great hurry.

73

Hsü Chieh gallops offstage, whipping his horse.
Enter a standard-bearer.

STANDARD-
BEARER His Lordship summons you into court.

Enter a crowd of officials and soldiers and some runners. Enter Hai
Jui, wearing a silk cap and red gown.

HAI JUI *recites*
I have received the imperial decree,
ordering the execution.
I shall eliminate the traitors
and set up proper standards.

Attendants, bring out the two condemned prisoners, Hsü Ying and
Wang Ming-yu. The day of execution has arrived.

Enter soldiers leading Hsü Ying and Wang Ming-yu, both bound.

HAI JUI Hsü Ying, Wang Ming-yu: the imperial decree has been handed down
calling for the sentence to be carried out. You are to be executed
forthwith. *signs writ of execution* You two villains!
recites
You disregarded the law of the country
and used that law for your advantage.
We shall make an example of you,
inspiring greedy people to reform.

HSÜ YING
WANG MING-YU Spare our lives, Your Worship. *they kowtow*

HAI JUI Take them away. They will be executed at the appointed time.

The soldiers lead Hsü Ying and Wang Ming-yu offstage.
Enter Tai Feng-hsiang's standard-bearer.

STANDARD-
BEARER I bring an imperial decree.

Drums and music. Enter Tai Feng-hsiang and Hsü Chieh, together.

TAI FENG-HSIANG By decree of his majesty the emperor, the Ying T'ien Governor Hai
Jui is dismissed from office and retired from public service. Let all
know that the new Ying T'ien Governor is Tai Feng-hsiang.

HAI JUI Long, long live the emperor. I would like to ask the great commissioner what transgression I have committed, that I should be stripped
of my rank and retired?

TAI FENG-HSIANG Officials at court have accused you of oppressing the common people and abusing the gentry.

HAI JUI What!
sings
The gentry are ruthless and overbearing,
the common people impoverished;
like wolves and tigers, the gentry
create an empty wilderness.
To speak of oppressing them is truly
utter nonsense,
and to degrade me
is most unreasonable and most unfair!

May I ask the great commissioner on what day the newly appointed governor will arrive here to take up office?

TAI FENG-HSIANG I am Tai Feng-hsiang himself. How do you do, Lord Hai.

HAI JUI How do you do, Lord Tai. Since you have arrived to take up your duties, I would like to say a few words to you.

TAI FENG-HSIANG Please do.

HAI JUI *sings*
The greatest evil in Kiangnan is the gentry,
who seize the people's land,
make agriculture difficult.
These injuries must be corrected.
Only the land's return can keep the peace.

TAI FENG-HSIANG Silence! It is precisely because you have oppressed the gentry by making them give back land, terrorized the common people, and badly mistreated the gentry, that the Emperor has dismissed you.
sings
One's relative rank or status in life
is a predestined matter.
It is entirely appropriate
that the masses should have a bitter time.
The distinction between good and bad
is precisely that between manual and mental labour.
You have studied the sacred books of Confucius:
that you should tyrannize the common folk
and treat a man with cruelty,

75

and even oppress the gentry,
is very wrong.

HAI JUI Who is wrong?

TAI FENG-HSIANG You are the one.

HAI JUI Silence!
sings
You say the common people are tyrannized,
but do you know the gentry injures them?
Much is made at court of the gentry's oppression,
but do you know of the poverty
endured by the common people?
You pay lip service to the principle
that the people are the roots of the state.
But officials still oppress the masses
while pretending to be virtuous men.
They act wildly as tigers
and deceive the emperor.
If your conscience bothers you,
you know no peace by day or night.

TAI FENG-HSIANG How do you have the gall to open your mouth and scold other men?
You make me furious.

HSÜ CHIEH Gentlemen, why don't both of you stop quarrelling and be more
agreeable? Kang-feng, some time ago I gave you some good advice.
I urged you not to stir up everyone's anger and not to cheat the gen-
try, but you would not listen. Now you are dismissed from office
and leaving here, and I have a few words for you.
sings
In your period of middle age,
your faculties remain acute.
You have tasted bitterness for several decades now.
You have been overzealous
in applying the law.
In your prejudice and radicalism you injure people.
The last time we talked, our conversation was unpleasant;
This time you have fallen,
and far-reaching changes have occurred.
I advise you to cultivate and refine yourself,
and if you get a post again,
do not indulge yourself like this.

76

HAI JUI Oh, Grand Tutor Hsü!

sings

The Grand Tutor's words are completely lacking in thought.
Hai Jui is dismissed from office,
but with a fragrant reputation.
As a man, I am on the inside
what I appear to be on the outside.
To secretly conspire for the downfall of another
is a dishonourable deed.

HSÜ CHIEH Who has secretly conspired?

HAI JUI You have!

sings

You have been at court
and held state power in your hands.
You talked of ethics, explained Confucius and Mencius,
and related details of the former kings.
Your sons who lived in the country
seized land and property.
abducted women, profferred bribes,
and acted altogether without conscience.
But suddenly you found a crafty way
to pull the wool over our sovereign's eyes,
and you have falsely accused the common people
of being the wolves and tigers.
You say the gentry are being victimized
and are unable to speak out,
but you can hardly escape
the hatred of all the people.
Where will you hide now?
I, Hai Jui, have lost my black silk cap,
but my conscience is clear.
One day I shall be an official again
and once again the law
will be enforced with rectitude.

HSÜ CHIEH You are so obstinate that there is nothing more to be said.

STANDARD-
BEARER The appointed time has arrived. Please give the order to carry out
the punishment.

TAI FENG-HSIANG

HSÜ CHIEH *alarmed* What punishment?

77

HAI JUI I have already received the imperial decree. Hsü Ying and Wang Ming-yu are to be executed forthwith.

HSÜ CHIEH What! *starts, pales, and begins to tremble*

TAI FENG-HSIANG Order the execution to be stopped.

HAI JUI Order the execution to go ahead.

TAI FENG-HSIANG The newly-appointed governor orders that the punishment be stopped.

HAI JUI The present governor orders that the execution go ahead.

TAI FENG-HSIANG Lord Hai, you cannot kill them.

HAI JUI Why not?

TAI FENG-HSIANG I have received personal instructions from Secretary of State Li and Inspector Feng that in deference to Grand Tutor Hsü's advanced age and his service to his country, Hsü Ying is to be reprieved. We are just awaiting the imperial decree.

HAI JUI Where is the imperial decree?

TAI FENG-HSIANG The imperial decree is following us and will arrive later.

HAI JUI And for the moment?

TAI FENG-HSIANG For the moment, I am issuing the order that in accordance with the instructions from the secretary of state and the inspector, a reprieve is to be granted.

HAI JUI You cannot go issuing orders.

TAI FENG-HSIANG Why not?

HAI JUI I still have not handed over to you. The Great Seal and the Arrow of Authority are still in my hands, so how can you issue any orders?

TAI FENG-HSIANG If this is the case, then please hand them over now.

HAI JUI Absolutely not. I have the imperial decree ordering me to go ahead with the punishment. When the execution is over, then I shall hand over to you.

78

TAI FENG-HSIANG   What! Lord Hai!
sings
To disobey an imperial edict is no small crime.
You may lose your life and have your entire clan
wiped out before your eyes.
You should respect the Grand Tutor's great age.
Do not succumb to your urges
or you will later regret it.

HAI JUI   Ha ha!
sings
I have received imperial authority
for this beheading.
The execution will of course
proceed forthwith.
How can one in office
heed special circumstances?
Even if punishment follows,
it is of no concern to me.

TAI FENG-HSIANG   Do you not even fear the misfortune of being killed as a result?

HAI JUI   A real man stands with his head held high and his feet planted firmly on the ground. How could I fear the misfortune of losing my life and bend the law according to my personal feelings? To do so would be to bring shame on myself as a man whose conduct was not pure and incorruptible. *grasping the Arrow of Authority* Standard-bearer, order the executions carried out.

STANDARD-
BEARER   *accepting the arrow* It will be done.

Exit the standard-bearer. Three shots of a cannon are heard. Hsü Chieh collapses on the ground; Tai Feng-hsiang becomes alarmed and flustered. Hai Jui holds up the Great Seal.

HAI JUI   Lord Tai, here is the Great Seal. Now, I shall hand over to you. I shall leave now.

Amazed and confused, Tai Feng-hsiang stands absolutely rigid. Hai Jui offers him the Great Seal again. The curtain falls.

ENTIRE CAST   *sings*
Heaven is cold, the earth is freezing,
and the wind whistles mournfully.
The thoughts of all the people
go with this official as he leaves.
Father Hai returns south
and we cannot stop him. We burn incense for the Living Buddha
of all the people.

79

2 The role of 'Hai Jui's Dismissal' in China's Cultural Revolution

The Charges

The first criticism of *Hai Jui's Dismissal* was widely hailed by the
official organs of the Chinese Communist Party as the first shot fired
in the Great Proletarian Cultural Revolution in China.[1] The purpose
of this chapter is to place Wu Han's drama in meaningful perspective
by noting the political environment in which it was written and by
discussing chronologically the series of events related to this drama,
which culminated in what many commentators have described as the
most crucial power struggle in the history of the Chinese Communist
Party.

The Great Proletarian Cultural Revolution has often been regarded
by Western analysts as a strictly political confrontation, having little
or no relation to the cultural sphere. It would be futile to dwell on
the distinction between the cultural and political aspects of the Cultural Revolution, as in China the two are inextricably related. Nevertheless, there are two points which should be stated clearly at this
time, both of which will be further amplified in the ensuing discussion.
The first is that although the Cultural Revolution did indeed, after
August 1966, become a fight for supremacy among competing elements within the Chinese Communist Party, there is no denying that
in the early stages it was waged almost exclusively within the cultural
sphere, involving plays, fables, essays, short stories, journalism, and
films. *Jen Min Jih Pao,* April-June 1966, is obsessed with the cultural
scene. An editorial in this newspaper on June 2, 1966, describing the
writers then under attack, stated, "On the cultural front, they have
worked to let emperors and kings, generals and prime ministers,
scholars and beauties, foreign idols and dead men dominate the stage."
On June 4, the same paper elaborated, "Your poisonous products
filled our newspapers, radio, magazines, books, textbooks, lectures,
literary works, films, plays, operas and ballads, fine arts, music, dancing." Again, on June 8, "We criticize the bourgeois conception of
history, bourgeois academic theories, pedagogy, journalism, and
theories of art and literature, and all bad plays, films, and works of
literature and art." In this sense the Cultural Revolution may be seen
as the latest stage of a campaign against writers and intellectuals which
has continued unabated ever since Mao Tse-tung enunciated his thesis
that all art and literature has a class character. According to this thesis

83

any art or literature not explicitly serving the interests of the workers, peasants, and soldiers must of necessity serve the interests of the exploiting classes.[2] The anti-Hu Feng movement of 1955 may then be seen as the direct historical antecedent of the Cultural Revolution.

The second point to be stressed, however, illustrates the futility of attempting to press the distinction between culture and politics too far. It will be clearly demonstrated below that although literature has been the vehicle through which the elements attacked in the initial stages of the Cultural Revolution had previously waged their own attacks on Mao Tse-tung, important aspects of Chinese foreign and domestic policy were from the beginning the real issues in dispute. The realm of art and literature has always been seen as a forum for class struggle in Communist China, and in the course of the Current Great Proletarian Cultural Revolution, it should not be surprising that *Liberation Army Daily,* the theoretical journal of the Chinese Liberation Army, should warn readers that the "enemies without guns" are far more deadly than any armed adversaries.[3]

The controversy raised by the criticism of Wu Han's drama in November of 1965 led directly to all the events which have transpired since. This is not at all to imply that *Hai Jui's Dismissal* caused the intra-party political dispute which was to follow. There is good reason to believe that the Mao and Liu lines had been in contention within the Chinese Communist Party at least since the "Hundred Flowers Campaign" of 1957.[4] Contrary to the beliefs of many China scholars, there is no clear evidence linking Liu Shao-ch'i with the opposition to Mao at the Lushan Plenum of 1959. Yet there is equally no evidence to the contrary, and whatever the role played by Liu personally, it is quite clear that the party was badly split from 1959 on as a result of the Mao-P'eng confrontation. Franz Schurmann put forward persuasive circumstantial evidence in the October 1966 issue of the *New York Review of Books* to indicate that Mao and Liu fell out only in early 1966, over the twin issues of opposition to the United States in Vietnam and a reconciliation with the Soviet Union.

Whatever the role Liu may have played in the years prior to 1966, it is absolutely clear that the substantial elements within the CCP leadership who continued to favour P'eng Teh-huai after the latter's dismissal in 1959 enjoyed a wide following among the intellectuals. Wu Han and his cronies did not "lead the forces of reaction." Rather they were allied with and working for much more powerful men. It will be clearly shown below that Mao made a number of attempts to initiate rectification campaigns against his adversaries in the fields of literature and art prior to 1965. In no case was he able to move the party apparatus to action. He was finally successful in launching his rectification campaign, now called the Cultural Revolution, only when he began to direct a concerted campaign against the Peking Municipal Party Committee from his stronghold in Shanghai. The campaign began to take shape with the attack on Wu Han, which was shortly extended to the entire Peking Committee. Ultimately Mao successfully went to the population at large and employed his immense personal prestige to enlist their support in attacking the Communist Party, over which he no longer exercised control.

The charges levelled against Wu amounted to charges of treason. As criticism of Wu grew more widespread, various colleagues who had either co-authored articles with him or sought to defend him at some point were implicated. Within a matter of months, a number of important political figures within the Chinese Communist Party had been attacked as the strategists standing behind the supposedly anticommunist writers. After a deluge of attacks on a wide variety of plays, films, essays, dramas, and anecdotes, the official charge was made that the traitors had their base in the Peking Municipal Party Committee.[5]

Although a number of Western commentators have recognized that *Hai Jui's Dismissal* sparked the current struggle, the actual content of the play has never to my knowledge been presented in its entirety to readers in the English language, and its political significance has never been analysed anywhere else but in the Chinese press. It is for this reason that I have translated the entire text here. The remainder of this chapter consists of a chronological survey of events from the origins of the Cultural Revolution until the end, in July 1966, of what might be called the literary phase of the struggle.

On June 19, 1959, an essay entitled "Hai Jui Scolds the Emperor" appeared in the pages of *Jen Min Jih Pao,* under the name of Liu Mien-chih. This was a pen-name used by Wu Han.[6] The article concerned the same Hai Jui who appears in the drama translated here, a genuine historical figure who served the Chia Ching Emperor in sixteenth-century China. The author emphasized the fact that in traditional China it was almost unheard of that any official should criticize the emperor, and expressed great joy at having discovered an historical official who actually possessed the courage to do so. With the advantage of hindsight and a considerable body of supporting evidence, we can now say with reasonable assurance that Wu Han's publication of this article was directly related to another event which occurred less than a month later.

On July 14, 1959, P'eng Teh-huai, then China's Minister of National Defence, sent a letter to Mao Tse-tung in which he articulated his opposition to the CCP general line, the Great Leap Forward, and the People's Communes.[7] In August of 1959 the Eighth Plenary Session of the Eighth Central Committee was held at Lushan in Kiangsi Province. At the Lushan Conference, an historic confrontation took place in which Marshal P'eng Teh-huai is alleged, with the aid of several high-ranking supporters within the party, to have launched a full assault on the leadership of Mao Tse-tung, the Great Leap Forward (charging it with failure), and the People's Commune movement.[8] P'eng Teh-huai was Minister of Defence at the time, and it is surmised that he and Mao may have clashed over much more than the Great Leap Forward and the People's Communes. There is, for example, reason to believe that P'eng and Mao had serious differences over the issue of the modernization of the Chinese People's Liberation Army and the acquisition of nuclear weapons in particular. This speculation is based on a combination of facts. Mao's decision to acquire nuclear weapons for China appears to have been made after receiving only minimal Soviet support during the Quemoy-Matsu crisis. Prior to the Lushan Conference, P'eng Teh-huai had been touring Eastern Europe and had been in close contact with Soviet leaders.[9] An analysis of the Sino-Soviet dispute is beyond the scope of this study, but considering that the conflict was developing in 1959, it should be noted that P'eng Teh-huai has been regarded as a pro-Soviet element within the CCP,[10] that after his dismissal he was defended by Nikita Khrushchov,[11] and that it has even been suggested that he may have divulged secret information to the Soviet leaders during his 1959 tour of Europe.[12]

In any case, Mao was able to withstand the challenge of P'eng Teh-huai and his supporters, and the latter were all dismissed from their posts by a special resolution of the Lushan Conference.[13] During this period and in the years immediately following, Wu Han's writings began to dwell on the exploits of Hai Jui and to praise him for having the courage to scold the emperor. Following the dismissal of the "Right Opportunist Clique" (as P'eng and his followers are now classified by the CCP), Wu Han began to extol the virtue and courage of Hai Jui after the latter's criticisms of and struggles against tyrants had resulted in his being dismissed from office. This is clearly one of the main themes of *Hai Jui's Dismissal,* a play on which, according to the preface, Wu Han began work almost immediately after the Lushan Conference. Two secondary themes, that of returning land to its rightful owners, and that of the opposition by honest officials to tyrants who had usurped power, were also stressed by Wu Han.

On September 21, 1959, Wu Han published another article in *Jen Min Jih Pao,* entitled "On Hai Jui." This article was widely interpreted as lauding P'eng Teh-huai.[14] Once more the theme of courage in the face of dismissal from office was stressed, and Wu Han called for a modern Hai Jui who would understand the people, lead them, and fight against modern bureaucratism in the same way that the historical Hai Jui had fought against the "feudal" gentry. In 1959 Wu Han also gathered together a collection of short stories he had published years earlier and republished them in a collection entitled *Javelin-Throwing.* This volume was also later criticized in the course of the Cultural Revolution. In the most important criticism later made of Wu Han, it was charged that *Hai Jui's Dismissal* was a prelude for all the anti-party literature in the years that followed.[15]

Hai Jui's Dismissal was first published in January 1961 in *Peking Literature and Art.* In March of the same year, Teng T'o[16] began a series of articles entitled "Evening Chats at Yenshan" which appeared in *Frontline* and the *Peking Daily.* As long as it continued to be published, "Evening Chats at Yenshan" constituted a series of bitingly satirical and sarcastic articles which lampooned Mao Tse-tung personally, in a manner which in most cases could not even be described as subtle.[17] When the Cultural Revolution was launched late in 1965, it was stated that the period of June to July, 1961, had constituted a major campaign by "Right Opportunist" writers to upset the results of the Lushan Conference.[18] One article by Wu Han, which had appeared on June 7, 1961, was particularly singled out for criticism.[19] In this article, Wu praised Yu Chien, another historical figure who had been dismissed from office. Moreover, he stated that Yu Chien had been rehabilitated and had returned to power as Secretary of War (the equivalent of Minister of National Defence).[20]

On October 10, 1961, the column "Notes from Three-Family Village" was initiated in the magazine *Frontline.* This column was jointly written by Wu Han, Teng T'o, and Liao Mo-sha.[21] By the spring of 1966, "Three-Family Village" had become a household word throughout China.[22] The expression referred to the newspaper column on one level, but on another and more common level it came to denote the three authors mentioned above, and by extension their supporters and sympathizers as well. On May 21, 1966, an article in Shanghai's *Liberation Daily* traced the origin of the name "Three-Family Village" to a poem by a Sung poet, Lu Yu, concerning a high official who had lost his post and was spending his last days in a place called Three-Family Village.[23]

The Twenty-second Congress of the Communist Party of the Soviet Union was convened in October 1961. The following month saw a proliferation of satirical material by the "Three-Family Village" group. On November 10, Teng's article "Great Empty Talk" appeared. Liao

Mo-sha published two articles on November 21. One, entitled "Where-in Lies Confucius' Greatness," characterized Confucius as a democrat. The second article was entitled "Jokes about Being Afraid of Ghosts" and was interpreted as supporting "revisionism." On November 26, Teng T'o published "Two Foreign Fables" in his regular column "Evening Chats at Yenshan," which was carried in the *Peking Evening News.* Teng was later accused of having used this article to attack the CCP policy of self-reliance. Between 1961 and 1963, Teng T'o alone wrote at least four separate articles on the theme of virtuous officials in Chinese history who were dismissed from office when they refused to compromise their principles.[24]

"On Waves," an article by Wu Han which appeared on January 1, 1962, was later interpreted by the foremost spokesman of the Cultural Revolution as the signal that the "Three-Family Village" forces intended to sweep everything before them in 1962.[25] In the February 4 instalment of "Evening Chats at Yenshan," Teng T'o wrote,

The bitter cold of the north wind will soon come to an end. In its stead a warm east wind will blow and a thaw will soon set in on this earth.[26]

Later it was charged that the use of the word "thaw" was a deliberate borrowing of the vocabulary used by the "Khrushchov revisionist clique against Stalin."[27] On March 29, 1962, Teng published an article entitled "In Defence of Li San-tsai."[28] Again the theme was that of a "good official" dismissed from office during the Ming Dynasty. In the most important criticism of "Three-Family Village" in 1966, the purpose of "defending" Li was questioned, since he had been dead for four hundred years and it was quite obvious that no one was attacking him.[29] It was also charged in 1966 that Li San-tsai was really a villain and that Teng T'o had whitewashed his character for his own political purposes.[30]

It appears that Mao Tse-tung and his supporters launched a counter attack against their critics during the Tenth Plenary Session of the Eighth Central Committee, held in September of 1962.[31] Mao used this conference as a forum from which to issue a plea that the class struggle never be forgotten and that "Right Opportunist" tendencies among the cadres be combatted.[32] Significantly, Teng T'o abandoned "Evening Chats at Yenshan" almost immediately after the Tenth Plenary Session.[33] This action appeared to be a signal for retreat on the part of "Three-Family Village." The three partners entered a period of decline and during 1963 and 1964 Liao Mo-sha was subjected to continuous public criticism because of his article "There Is No Harm in Ghost Plays."[34] It was later noted by Wu Han's chief attacker that the self-criticism published by Liao Mo-sha in this period was repeated almost word for word by Wu Han when he himself was attacked at a later date.[35]

On June 5, 1964, Lu Ting-i, Director of the Propaganda Department of the Central Committee of the Chinese Communist Party, made an important speech in which he linked ghost themes in Peking Opera dramas with support for "Khrushchov Revisionists." [36] In the course of this speech, Lu made an obvious reference to the above-mentioned article by Liao Mo-sha.[37] In July, "Notes from Three-Family Village" was discontinued.

Mao Tse-tung is said to have called for the launching of a new wave of criticism against reactionary bourgeois ideology at a meeting of the central leadership of the Chinese Communist Party in September 1965.[38] Shortly afterward he disappeared from public view and was not seen from November 1965 until May 1966. It is possible that Mao was already experiencing difficulty with the leadership in Peking and that he planned the early stages of the Cultural Revolution in Shanghai. This speculation is based on a combination of noteworthy facts. The beginning of Mao's absence from public view coincided with the publication of Yao Wen-yuan's attack on Wu Han. This article initiated the Cultural Revolution. In a very short time, the Cultural Revolution began to assume the character of an attack on Peking party officials by their counterparts in Shanghai. Not until the Peking Municipal Party Committee and its official organs were reeling under heavy attack did Mao reappear in public. What is known for sure is that when the first banner of the Cultural Revolution was raised, it was raised in Shanghai. Moreover, several CCP documents have indicated that Mao's hand guided the Cultural Revolution from the first.[39] The remainder of the chronology presented here shows quite clearly that the call for the Cultural Revolution was taken up only belatedly in Peking and that when the purges began in 1966 they were directed almost exclusively against Peking government and party officials.

The Great Proletarian Cultural Revolution was launched on November 10, 1965, with the publication of an article in the Shanghai newspaper *Wen Hui Pao*,[40] criticizing Wu Han. Written by Yao Wen-yuan and entitled "On the New Historical Drama, *Hai Jui's Dismissal*," the article became the model for almost all the criticisms later levelled against the assorted works of "Three-Family Village" and other writers of a similar bent. Yao charged that Wu Han was using historical characters in order to satirize contemporary people and events, that he was denying the basic thesis of Mao Tse-tung which holds that only the people are the motive force of history, and instead substituting the actions of an honest and upright "saviour" as an antidote

89

to all the hardships which plagued the peasants. Further, he accused Wu of desiring

to replace the state theory of Marxism-Leninism with the state theory of the landlords and bourgeoisie. He wishes to replace the theory of class struggle with the theory of class harmony.

Finally, Yao raises the fact that in the preface to *Hai Jui's Dismissal,* Wu Han had suggested that there were things to be learned from the old histories and that the life of Hai Jui was worthy of study today. Noting that the two most important themes of the play were the return of the land to its rightful owners and the redress of grievances, Yao asked two very pointed questions. First, was it land reform the readers were to learn about, or something else? In the words of Yao,

The peasants of our country have already realized socialism, possess everything, and have established the great People's Communes. Return to whom? The landlords? The peasants? Can one say that, on the road of socialism, our five hundred million peasants need to study the lesson of "returning the land"?

Or, second, were readers to learn from this play some lesson having to do with redressing injustices? Again, Yao Wen-yuan answers his own rhetorical question:

Our country is one which has achieved the state power of the proletariat. If we speak of "redressing injustices" at a time when the proletariat and all the oppressed have been delivered from the hell on earth of the exploiting classes, if the landlords and bourgeoisie have been smashed, how can it be said ... that there are any injustices to redress? If, in the contemporary situation, he wants us to learn about the "redress of injustices," I would like to ask, in the final analysis, which class has suffered the "injustice" and how is it to be "redressed"?

The fact that Yao Wen-yuan's article quickly became a basic manual for the prosecution of the Cultural Revolution and was probably the most widely quoted document in China during 1966 has led to some interesting speculation on the part of non-Chinese observers. The unique prestige which the essay has enjoyed was linked with statements in Chinese documents to the effect that Mao's guiding hand was behind the Cultural Revolution from the beginning,[41] and was presented as evidence that Yao Wen-yuan was in fact Mao Tse-tung.[42] This speculation, however, appeared for several reasons to have little basis in fact. On November 22, 1966, Yao Wen-yuan was named a member of the Cultural Revolution Group,[43] the body officially described as "an organ of power of the Cultural Revolution."[44] He was also identified as the chief editor of the Shanghai newspapers *Wen Hui Pao* and *Liberation Daily* at the time his essay appeared.[45] Furthermore, he delivered at least one major public address,[46] and was photographed in public with Mao.[47] The period of the Cultural Revolution was one in which Yao Wen-yuan vaulted from relative obscurity to a position in the inner circles of Chinese leadership. He became the youngest member of the new Chinese Politburo when on April 28, 1969, he was elected to this select body by the First Plenary Session of the Ninth Central Committee of the Chinese Communist Party. Had the Taiwanese theorists who were so quick to equate Yao with Mao been more diligent in their research, they would have discovered that although Yao had yet to achieve wide repute, he had long been involved in rectification campaigns against certain members of the Chinese intellectual community. He gained a certain amount of local prominence in Shanghai during the anti-Hu Feng campaign of 1955. During the anti-rightist campaign of 1957, Yao came to lead the attack on Shanghai writers. In the 1960 campaign against "revisionist writers," Yao Wen-yuan fired the opening shot with an article entitled, "Criticize Pa Jen's Theory of Human Nature." Pa Jen was at that time Director of the Peking People's Literature Publishing House and had formerly been an ambassador to Indonesia.

Not until November 29, 1965, did the *Peking Daily* reprint Yao Wen-yuan's article. This delay of almost twenty days formed the basis of a later attack against the *Peking Daily* and the magazine *Frontline* by *Red Flag,* the theoretical journal of the Chinese Communist Party.[48] The editors of these two publications were accused of criticizing the publication of the article in Shanghai.[49] It has also been charged that the *Peking Daily* and *Frontline,* together with the *Peking Evening News,* systematically attempted to stifle a growing wave of criticism against Wu Han.[50]

December 12, 1965, marked a shift in tactics by the members of "Three-Family Village." On this date, *Frontline* and *Peking Daily* both published an article by Hsiang Yang-sheng, entitled "From *Hai Jui's Dismissal* to the Theory of Inheriting Old Ethical Values." This article was the first in a series of criticisms and self-criticisms which were later identified as "phoney" attempts to deflect the growing criticism of Wu Han and "Three Family Village" before the political purposes of the writers were exposed.[51] Hsiang Yang-sheng appeared to chastise Wu Han quite thoroughly, but it should be noted that he treated Wu Han's errors purely as a case of bad historiography and completely ignored the political implications raised by Yao Wen-yuan's article of a month before. The questions asked by Yao and

91

quoted earlier in this chapter concerning whether Wu Han was actually propagating "return of the land" and "redress of injustices" in contemporary China were not explored. The key question of a link between Wu's writings and the 1959 Lushan Conference was also avoided. Wu Han published a self-criticism in the *Peking Daily* on December 27. In his confession, Wu criticized himself for having forgotten the class struggle, ignored class contradictions in history, and falsified the real character of Hai Jui. Completely ignoring what he had said in the preface to *Hai Jui's Dismissal,* however, Wu claimed that his writings constituted only "drama for the sake of drama" and that they had absolutely no significance for contemporary situations. *Jen Min Jih Pao* reprinted Wu's self-criticism on December 30.[52]

In early 1966 a number of allegedly anti-socialist literary works and their authors were subjected to criticism,[53] although the attack on Wu Han grew in intensity and continued to be the main focus of the Cultural Revolution. On January 8 a stage play entitled *Hsieh Yao-huan,* written by T'ien Han,[54] was described as a "big poisonous weed" by *Jen Min Jih Pao.* The *Peking Daily* published a second self-criticism by Wu Han on January 12. In this article, Wu Han expressed gratitude to Hsiang Yang-sheng for pointing out his errors, and admitted that his articles had lacked adequate class analysis. One of Yao Wen-yuan's most central themes in his attack on "Three-Family Village" is the fact that the three partners and the publications under their control, when faced with attack, have consistently criticized themselves for forgetting the class struggle. Yao maintains that, on the contrary, they have constantly and consciously waged a class struggle against the CCP. Within a few months it was disclosed that Hsiang Yang-sheng was a pseudonym employed by Teng T'o.[55] On January 8, an article by one Li Tung-shih was published in the *Peking Daily,* entitled "A Comment on Comrade Wu Han's Conception of History." The article was interpreted by Chi Pen-yü, a leading critic of "Three-Family Village," as describing "the 'guiding' thought in Wu Han's *Hai Jui's Dismissal* as a kind of viewpoint in appraising historical characters." At no point in the article, said Chi Pen-yü, was *Hai Jui's Dismissal* "admitted to be an anti-party and anti-socialist product." Li Tung-shih is said to have been a pseudonym for Li Chi, the Director of the Propaganda Department of the Peking Municipal Party Committee.[56]

The first significant reverberation in the political realm occurred on March 29, when P'eng Chen, the mayor of Peking, eighth ranking man in the Chinese Communist Party, and long a confidante of President Liu Shao-ch'i,[57] disappeared from public view.[58] Although P'eng was not seen in public after this date, the political implications were not fully appreciated until he lost his position as first secretary of the

Peking Municipal Committee of the CCP in early June. Just prior to P'eng's dismissal, on May 21, *Jen Min Jih Pao* stated that someone more powerful must have been standing behind the members of "Three-Family Village," shielding and supporting them. The paper demanded that this person be identified.

In April and May the attack on Wu Han reached a level of unprecedented ferocity. "The Reactionary Nature of 'Hai Jui Scolds the Emperor' and *Hai Jui's Dismissal*," by Chi Pen-yu, and "'Hai Jui Scolds the Emperor' and *Hai Jui's Dismissal* Are Two Big Anti-Party, Anti-Socialist Poisonous Weeds," by Kuan Feng and Lin Chieh, were two key articles published early in April by *Red Flag*. The latter was particularly significant in that it formally charged Wu Han with the crimes hinted at by Yao Wen-yuan's article. For example, the two authors are explicit in their allegations that Wu Han's writings concerning Hai Jui were directly connected with the Lushan Conference. The formal charge is made for the first time that Wu Han's real intention was to scold the Chinese Communist Party and its Central Committee. Wu Han is accused of singing the praises of the Right Opportunist elements who had been dismissed from office, encouraging them not to lose heart because of their failure and urging them to "reassume political power and restore capitalism."

Also in April, Wu Han was subjected to a widening range of criticism in a series of increasingly unsophisticated articles printed by *Jen Min Jih Pao.* His family background and class origins were thoroughly scrutinized in the pages of the newspaper.[59] His educational history was also examined.[60] On April 13, an article in *Jen Min Jih Pao* accused Wu Han of being a devoted follower of Hu Shih, and a fervent admirer and cultural servant of the USA. The title of another article appearing in the same newspaper on April 27 speaks for itself: "Wu Han: Strategist for the Chiang Family Monarchists and Helper of American Imperialism." *Red Flag,* on April 29, carried a long article attacking *Javelin-Throwing,* the collection of Wu Han's satirical essays mentioned earlier. It was alleged that this volume was intended to provide "Right Opportunists" with a blueprint for overthrowing socialism and restoring capitalism.[61]

At the same time, the attack on Wu Han now grew into an onslaught against the entire "Three-Family Village" superstructure. On April 16, *Frontline* and the *Peking Daily* both published an article entitled "A Criticism of 'Three-Family Village' and *Evening Chats at Yenshan.*" The editors of the two publications engaged in some very mild self-criticism, stating that their "minds were influenced by bourgeois and feudal ideas."[62] Yao Wen-yuan later charged that "Three-Family Village" had been in complete control of the *Peking Daily, Peking Evening*

93

News and *Frontline,* and that their crimes had not been the result of any mistakes, but had on the contrary constituted a well planned and well co-ordinated campaign against the party over a long period of time.[63] Yao reminded his readers that at an earlier stage, Teng T'o had penned a fraudulent criticism of Wu Han under the name of Hsiang Yang-sheng in order to divert the main force of the attack from "Three-Family Village." He charged *Peking Daily* and *Frontline* with employing the same tactics.

The month of May brought a flurry of attacks on "Three-Family Village." On May 8 the *Liberation Daily* in Shanghai published two militant articles[64] attacking *Peking Daily* and *Frontline* for the reasons stated in the previous paragraph.[65] Two days later the same paper printed an extensive condemnation by Yao Wen-yuan, entitled "On 'Three-Family Village': The reactionary Nature of 'Evening Chats at Yenshan' and 'Notes from Three-Family Village.'" Yao's latest article came to play a role in relation to "Three-Family Village" which was identical to that which his earlier article had played in relation to the writings of Wu Han. On May 11 an article appeared in *Red Flag,* further amplifying the extent of the control which "Three-Family Village" had exercised over *Peking Daily* and *Frontline.*[66] *Jen Min Jih Pao* of May 14 published an attack on Teng T'o,[67] and for the rest of the month there was scarcely an issue which did not carry several attacks on him. Finally, on May 25, the newly re-organized Peking Municipal Party Committee dismissed the editorial boards of *Peking Daily* and *Peking Evening News,* fired their director, Fan Chin, and suspended publication of *Frontline.*[68]

It was in June of 1966 that a series of major political repercussions occurred, moving the Cultural Revolution out of the literary sphere and into the arena of a serious political struggle within the Chinese Communist Party itself. On June 3 the Central Committee of the CCP decided to completely reorganize the Peking Municipal Party Committee.[69] It was at this time that Li Hsueh-feng was transferred from his post as first secretary of the North China Bureau of the CCP Central Committee to that of first secretary of the Peking Municipal Committee.[70] Wu Teh, first secretary of the CCP Kirin Provincial Committee, became second secretary of the Peking Municipal Committee.[71] At the same time Lu P'ing was dismissed from his posts as president of Peking University and secretary of the Peking University Party Committee.[72]

On June 4 *Jen Min Jih Pao* made the claim that "Three-Family Village" had had its roots right in the Peking Municipal Party Committee.[73] This was not an unreasonable charge, in view of the fact that the *Peking Daily* and *Frontline* were both organs of the Peking

Committee.[74] An editorial in *Liberation Army Daily* in Shanghai on June 6 made the direct accusation that "Three-Family Village" had been in constant close collusion with the Right Opportunists both before and after the Lushan Conference. The same editorial linked up "Hai Jui Scolds the Emperor," *Hai Jui's Dismissal*, "Evening Chats at Yenshan," "Notes From Three-Family Village," and the three publications *Frontline, Peking Daily*, and *Peking Evening News* as component parts of a sinister plot against the CCP. On June 17 an attack was launched against Ch'en Ch'i-t'ung, deputy director of the General Political Department of the People's Liberation Army, for an article he had written entitled "A Searching Anatomy."

Red Flag launched a two-pronged attack on July 1. On the one hand it accused "leading members of the former Peking Municipal Committee" of promoting revisionism. Simultaneously, it launched the first attack on Chou Yang.[75]

Lu Ting-i was removed from his position as director of the Propaganda Department of the Central Committee of the CCP on July 10, 1966, and replaced by T'ao Chu.[76] It has been suggested that action was taken against Lu because he procrastinated in carrying out Mao's directives on the Cultural Revolution.[77] The evidence for this view is based on the fact that until June neither *Jen Min Jih Pao* nor *Red Flag* had participated in the Cultural Revolution with a zeal comparable to that of *Wen Hui Pao, Liberation Daily*, and *Liberation Army Daily*. It is only by comparing these papers from January to June, 1966, that the difference can be appreciated. *Jen Min Jih Pao* seemed in April and May to be joining in the Cultural Revolution with great vigour. However, much of the material it printed was initiated in Shanghai. Both of the former publications were directly under the control of Lu Ting-i in his capacity as Director of Propaganda.[78] By July 11 a furious attack against Chou Yang was in progress, and during the remainder of July and most of August it rivalled in intensity the earlier campaign against Wu Han. The political struggles that occurred after August 1966 moved to even higher levels of the Chinese Communist Party, until eventually it resulted in conflict between the two top men. This phase of the Cultural Revolution is beyond the scope of the present study.

Evaluation of the Charges

In this chapter an attempt will be made to determine what it was that Wu Han was expressing in *Hai Jui's Dismissal* and other related writings from 1959 through the early 1960s. In order to do this, it will also be necessary to analyse the most important charges which have been brought against him and determine whether or not they are basically valid.

Prior to analysing the charges brought against Wu Han, there are certain observations which can be made simply on the basis of a reading of the play, together with other articles on Hai Jui and similar themes by the same author, and a representative collection of material penned by the other two members of "Three-Family Village." Ordinarily, it would be completely unjustifiable to hold one man responsible for the works of other contemporary writers. However, very substantial evidence has been brought forward to indicate that Wu Han was co-ordinating his efforts closely with those of Teng T'o and Liao Mo-sha. It has already been noted that "Notes from Three-Family Village" was jointly written by all three. In the last chapter, it was also pointed out that when Wu Han first came under attack, Teng T'o penned a sham criticism of Wu under a pseudonym. Moreover, in February 1961, after *Hai Jui's Dismissal* had been published, Liao Mo-sha published an open letter to Wu Han, congratulating him on "breaking through the door and dashing out ... in order to encourage people to greater efforts." [1] Therefore it seems perfectly valid to examine the writings of the latter two for themes identical or complementary to material appearing under Wu Han's name.

For the moment, let us by-pass the question whether or not *Hai Jui's Dismissal* harbours a genuine and deliberate attack on the Chinese Communist Party and Chairman Mao Tse-tung. Even had the play not been so interpreted, it is still likely that it would have been subjected to serious criticism in China. Even to a reader with only a rudimentary knowledge of communist ideology and the Marxist interpretation of history, it is immediately obvious that nearly all the important themes and ideas expressed here are anathema to Marxism-Leninism.

Wu Han begins by telling us that he uses the case of Hung A-lan to illustrate the class contradictions of the time. Yet in the play itself, the problems of Hung A-lan are clearly not solved through conflict involving any class contradictions. On the contrary, the solution of her problems depends entirely on the benevolence of an official who, Wu Han himself tells us, is entirely loyal to the "feudal" ruling class. The only meaningful class contradictions during the period in which the drama is set would have to be between the ruling class of "feudal" landlords on the one hand, and the peasantry on the other. Yet Wu Han has taken a member of the former class and portrayed him as the saviour of the latter class. Class contradictions appear to be completely solved once the land is returned to the peasants. "A promising future" lies ahead, even though the "feudal" system continues. Revolution would seem to be unnecessary under such circumstances. A few paragraphs after the reference to Hung A-lan, Wu writes of the "longing, affection, and friendship for Hai Jui" felt by the peasantry.

The dependence of the common people on the virtue of a saviour who emerges from the ranks of the ruling class is an important theme running through the entire drama. In the scene "A Mother's Counsel," it is said of the common people that since Hai Jui assumed office there has been a "living Buddha" for every household. The same term is used to describe Hai Jui when the entire cast assembles on stage at the play's close. The peasants remark that Hai Lung Wang has come to earth. This is almost tantamount to portraying Hai Jui as some form of superman. When Hai Jui finally brings justice to Hung A-lan and returns the land to the peasants, the peasants announce that when they go home they will have a portrait of Hai Jui painted which they will honour (the Chinese word is very close to "worship") morning and evening. It would be difficult to imagine anything more un-Marxist than the fawning, idolatrous worship of Hai Jui by the peasants in this play.

There are numerous other examples of ideas which simply cannot be reconciled with Marxism-Leninism. Hai Jui's unswerving devotion to the emperor is portrayed as a virtue. Yet it is absolutely basic to Chinese Communist ideology that the emperor, as the supreme authority in a system which exploited the peasants, was the enemy of the people. We see the glorification of traditional Confucian teachings in the description by Hsieh Shih of the upbringing she has given her son. In the same scene Hai Jui sings, "The resentment of the people / bubbles and boils; / their hatred will be hard to overcome." The idea that it should be overcome, in order to prevent the outbreak of revolt, would immediately be interpreted by any Marxist-Leninist as the propagation of "reformist" politics.

There are times when Wu Han's viewpoints appear so "reactionary" that it is scarcely possible for the reader to believe that his writings appeared in print in contemporary China. In his essay, "On Hai Jui,"[2]

97

Wu praises Hai Jui for the fact that his actions never betrayed any unseemly emotions and states that he patterned his standards on those of the ancient emperors. "Even when he beat his slaves," Wu tells us, "he never displayed any anger." Later in the same article, Wu Han introduces as evidence of Hai Jui's virtue the fact that Ho Liang-chün criticized Hai Jui only for attempting to implement his reform policies too rapidly. Ho Liang-chün was the greatest landlord in the Sungkiang-Suchow area during the period when Hai Jui governed there, and his father was the government tax collector.[3]

Although the discussion to this point shows quite clearly that Wu Han's thinking is incompatible with the basic tenets of Marxism, the instances cited so far certainly do not constitute any proof that the author was intentionally attacking the Chinese Communist Party or any of its leaders. Wu Han has never himself been a member of the CCP.[4] He was a member of the Democratic League.[5] It is certainly conceivable that his writings simply represent the ideas of a man whose understanding of Marxism never rose above a very low level. Indeed, this is essentially what Wu tells us in his two self-criticisms of late 1965 and early 1966.[6] The essence of his position at that time was that through lack of vigilance on his part, his mind was influenced by bourgeois ideology and he had forgotten the class struggle. It is therefore now necessary to examine the evidence for the much more serious charges which Wu Han's critics levelled against him, thus precipitating the Cultural Revolution.

Yao Wen-Yuan maintains that all the writings of Wu Han and "Three-Family Village" as a whole since 1959 were carefully planned and co-ordinated. Yao's articles criticizing Wu Han and "Three-Family Village" have become something akin to modern classics in the course of the Cultural Revolution. After Yao's initial article, literally scores of attacks appeared in the Chinese press. Very few, however, had new evidence to bring to light, and most simply parroted Yao. Given the prominence which the Chinese accorded his first essay, one is surprised at the lack of sophistication of much of its content. As will be shown, there are strong arguments which can be brought to bear in support of Yao Wen-yuan's contentions; nevertheless, his case and those later presented by many of his followers are considerably weakened by the fact that many of their charges are either utterly ludicrous or else altogether irrelevant. Furthermore, their sources are at times very dishonestly presented. This aspect of the attack will be considered before going on to some of the more concrete charges.

One of the flagrantly dishonest techniques employed by Yao Wen-yuan is that of citing quotations taken not only out of context, but frequently with no reference given.[7] Often, even a single word will appear in quotation marks in the middle of a paragraph which contains the most damning statements but which, with the exception of the one word quoted, has been composed entirely by Yao. As will be seen shortly, this was a technique which was carried to even greater lengths by later critics. Also, Yao has a habit of stringing together a whole series of highly questionable hypotheses, each of which is dependent on the validity of the one preceding it, and then arriving at a sweeping conclusion which simply cannot be justified on the basis of the evidence presented. For example, in his attack on "Three-Family Village," Yao quotes Teng T'o as having once written, "'everything' should be 'actively guided to facilitate its smooth development.'" Yao Wen-yuan's analysis of the meaning of these few words deserves to be quoted at some length as an apt example of his ability to construct a large case from very meagre materials.

"Everything," please note, including those dark, reactionary things that are anti-Party and anti-socialist ... By demanding that instead of blocking we should "facilitate the smooth development" of "everything," including anti-socialist things, was not Teng T'o clearly demanding that we should practice bourgeois liberalization and bend and surrender to the ill winds which were blowing at the time, the winds of "going it alone" [i.e., the restoration of individual economy] and of the extension of plots for private use and of free markets, the increase of small enterprises with sole responsibility for their own profits or losses, and the fixing of output quotas based on the household?[8]

Yao is also prone to lapse occasionally into the rather hysterical use of jargon.[9]

The above criticisms of Yao Wen-yuan, however, do not really deal with his central arguments. He levels one very basic charge against Wu Han which should now be carefully considered, since Yao chooses to base his case largely on this charge. He accuses Wu Han of having advocated the return of the land to the landlord class in contemporary China by falsifying history in his portrayal of Hai Jui. Yao maintains that the historical Hai Jui bore no resemblance whatever to the Hai Jui depicted in Wu Han's drama.

Yao's arguments on the historical questions raised by the play are on a much more sophisticated level than his other criticisms noted above. His main arguments will be summarized here and then evaluated. He cites Wu Han's constant reference in the play to the "people's lands" which have been seized by big landlords. Yao points out that an examination of Ming history will show that the lands seized at that time by big landlords had previously belonged to small and middle landlords. The system of tax evasion by big landlords existing at that time[10] had led to a situation in which big landlords became bigger and small landlords became progressively smaller. Yao claims that the demise of the small and middle landlord classes had a seriously adverse effect on the income of the state. Therefore, under the conditions prevailing at that time, he sees the return of the land as a benefit to the state and the emperor rather than as a benefit to the people. Yao advances his argument a step further by reasoning that since the records show that in the period in which the drama takes place, 90 per cent of the land was owned by landlords, any talk of returning land to the original owners must mean returning it to small and middle landlords. Moreover, Yao claims that according to the plan of the real Hai Jui, the land was not to be returned free of charge, but had to be re-purchased by the original owners. Obviously, the peasants could not afford to pay even if they had originally owned the land. On the basis of these facts, Yao argues that Wu Han is using his drama to propagate the return of the land to the landlords in contemporary China.

Yao quotes from a letter written by Hai Jui, in his capacity as Ying T'ien Governor, to Li Ch'ung-fang.[11] In this letter, Hai Jui says that he wants Li to return more than half the land in his possession. Otherwise, he says, the peasants will revolt and "you will lose control." He admonishes Li to be satisfied with the land he has and states that he is taking this action "only for your lasting peace." Since the return of the land was implemented only for the purpose of preventing a rebellion of the people, Yao asks how Wu Han can possibly suggest that Hai Jui was really concerned with solving the land problems of the tenant farmers.

The same analysis is applied to the memorial which Hai Jui sent to the Chia Ching Emperor. According to Yao's sources, Hai Jui's complaint to the emperor in this document was not that the plight of the people was difficult to bear. Rather, he was concerned that the money-lenders and millers were allowed to take their cut of the people's crops before the emperor's tax was applied. He suggested that the emperor's shortage of funds, which had resulted from the tax evasion system mentioned earlier, could be solved by taking the taxes first and then allowing the money-lenders to exact their interest from the people. Wu Han never ceases to eulogize Hai Jui for his virtue, honesty, and refusal to compromise his principles, and states that he stood on the side of the people against the large landlords. This point was later greatly amplified by Kuan Feng and Lin Chieh. They charge that Wu Han has translated the original memorial from Classical Chinese into modern and used his own translation as the basic source for his description of the memorial in "Hai Jui Scolds the Emperor" and *Hai Jui's Dismissal*. It is claimed that Wu Han's translation is entirely different from the original. Allegedly, some parts are taken out of context, some are entirely different from the ideas expressed in the original, and some are entirely figments of Wu Han's imagination.[12]

A very basic question occurs at this stage. Can Wu Han really be faulted for the bad characteristics of the real Hai Jui? Many dramas in both East and West have eulogized historical characters who were undoubtedly never as noble in real life as on the stage. Certainly, it need hardly be mentioned that "proletarian writers" in China imbue their characters with superhuman qualities as a matter of course. Hai Jui, to be sure, is drawn from the "feudal" ruling class, but that is a matter to be discussed separately below. The question for consideration here is whether a writer can legitimately be charged with harbouring malevolent intentions simply on the basis of having "whitewashed" an historical character for dramatic purposes. It seems that the key factor in this case would be the historical awareness of the audience watching the play. If those who saw a performance of *Hai Jui's Dismissal* were fully aware of the details of Hai's life, then the requirements for satire would be fulfilled, and Yao Wen-yuan's accusation of falsifying history would have some meaning. On the assumption, however, that the audience's acquaintance with Hai Jui's personal history would not be nearly so intimate as that of Wu Han, it would be reasonable to conclude that the message contained in what transpired on the stage would have a far more profound impact on the audience than would the facts of Hai Jui's real intentions four hundred years ago. In other words, to substantiate Yao's charges that Wu Han was advocating publicly the return of land to the landlords in contemporary China by depicting Hai Jui as an unceasing advocate of the restitution of land to the peasantry in Ming China, it must be conclusively shown that the Chinese public today is fully aware of the conditions of land tenure in China during the Ming dynasty and, further, that these conditions would be recalled to the mind of an audience by the events of the play.

Yao claims that in Ming times the peasantry had virtually no land and thus restoration could only mean restoration to landlords. But of what significance is this fact if it is not generally appreciated by the public watching the play? There cannot possibly be anyone in China today who is not thoroughly familiar with the collectivization of land which took place in the country during the 1950s. This was land which in the initial stages of the Chinese People's Republic had been owned by individual peasants. Thus it is very probable that Wu

Han's opposition to the People's Communes was indeed understood by his audiences, but understood because of their awareness of events in contemporary China rather than their knowledge of Ming land tenure or their perception of the "whitewashing" of Hai Jui by Wu Han. Similarly, the constant harping on the theme of "dismissal" could quite likely bring to the minds of many the dismissal of Marshal P'eng Teh-huai. It is at best doubtful that any of Wu's subtle historical changes concerning the dismissal of Hai Jui would be comprehended by a general audience.

The absurdity of Yao Wen-yuan's charges on this level may perhaps be best illustrated by constructing an hypothetical analogy in Western terms. Suppose a North American social critic, perhaps motivated by disgust with the inequities of distribution on this continent, were to produce a play about the exploits of Robin Hood in befriending the poor and protecting them against their oppressors. Let us then suppose further that after the play has been produced, the author is subjected to attack by a political enemy who accuses him of falsifying history and "whitewashing" the character of Robin Hood. Contrary to the popular conception, says the playwright's attacker, the real Robin Hood was a vicious thief who preyed on the public at large and was actually a lackey of the Sheriff of Nottingham. Therefore, by glorifying the character of Robin Hood, the author is actually subtly advocating the abuse of the poor. Yet if the conception the audience had of the historical Robin Hood derived entirely from the play they were watching, what possible relevance could the facts of history have for the author's political intentions? The critic in this hypothetical case would be making almost exactly the same charge that Yao Wen-yuan is making against Wu Han.

Perhaps anticipating some doubts about the relevance of his charge that Wu Han has falsified history, Yao Wen-yuan attempts to set out some criteria for defining the bounds within which an historical dramatist may operate:

Historical dramas need some artistic improvements and also require creativity. We definitely do not ask that new historical dramas be exactly according to history in all their details, but we must ask that a character's class standpoint and class relations fit historical fact.[13]

Nevertheless, he still seeks to embellish his case against Wu Han with the quibble that according to the official histories, the magistrate and prefect were neither executed nor discharged by Hai Jui. No one higher than a magistrate was discharged during the period in which Hai Jui served as Ying T'ien Governor. Yao also takes pains to point out that Hsü Ying was not really executed, but only exiled for ten years. This news, of course, comes with a somewhat lessened impact since Wu Han has already stated it in his preface, and fully explained his reasons for making the change.

Yao is quite concerned, too, about the fact that Hsü Ying's punishment was not really handled by Hai Jui at all, but by Kao Kung, the prime minister who had succeeded Hsü Chieh after securing the latter's dismissal. Again, Wu Han has already stated in his preface that he has cast Huang Chin and Tai Feng-hsiang in roles which are not strictly accurate historically. This practice not only appears perfectly reasonable for dramatic purposes, but also falls completely within the bounds set by Yao Wen-yuan himself in the quotation just cited. Yao reaches perhaps the lowest level of that part of his criticism based on historical analysis when he chides Wu Han for portraying Hai Jui as repairing the water control system on the Wusung River in one week. He holds that this would have been a physically impossible task, forgetting that "historical dramas need some artistic improvements and ... creativity." Yao could also perhaps be accused of forgetting that there can be no limits to the achievements of the people when properly motivated.[14]

Aside from the preceding array of charges concerning Wu Han's trifling with history, there is another charge which is also very weak. The reader cannot have helped noticing the emphasis throughout the play on Hai Jui's steadfast refusal to compromise his principles, regardless of the situation in which he finds himself. No matter who opposes him, he always stands his ground. Yao claims that this "individualism" identifies Hai Jui as a bourgeois hero. A proletarian hero, claims Yao, is always willing to modify his position according to the views of other people. If anyone in China ever applies the same standards of analysis to this statement that Yao Wen-yuan has applied to Wu Han's emphasis on the "return of the land," Yao himself could well become a victim of the Cultural Revolution. The people surrounding Hai Jui and opposing his policies were exclusively officials and gentry who quarrelled with his restrictions on their exploitation of the peasantry. Thus it is obvious that for Hai Jui to fulfil the requirements of a proletarian hero and submit to the views of others, he would have to adopt the policies of the biggest landlords. It might therefore be argued that Yao Wen-yuan is really using his attack on Wu Han as a vehicle to argue for the restoration of capitalism and landlordism!

Once Yao Wen-yuan's article had fired the first salvo of the Cultural Revolution, a proliferation of critics appeared in the pages of several Chinese daily newspapers and fortnightly magazines. Generally speaking, the charges levelled against Wu Han became ever graver and the evidence upon which they were based became ever flimsier. Two documents will be briefly noted here as examples of the level to which the

103

theoretical basis of the attack on Wu Han had sunk by April 1966.

On April 27 *Jen Min Jih Pao* published a lengthy article by Li Ssu-chün, entitled "Wu Han: Strategist for the Chiang Family Monarchists and Helper of American Imperialism." The basis for this sensational charge consists entirely of a collection of quotations from Chiang K'ai-shek, Wu Han, Hu Shih, and a number of American officials. Occasionally, the quotations express roughly similar ideas. The author quotes Chiang K'ai-shek, in *China's Destiny*, as saying that in the present period of Chinese history it is necessary for a small group of politicians and scholars to come forward and assume the responsibility of changing Chinese social customs. A statement by Wu Han is then taken from one of his essays, "Social Customs," arguing that only the educated group within the middle class can assume responsibility for changing social customs. An elitist and un-Maoist viewpoint this certainly is; proof of collusion with Chiang K'ai-shek it decidedly is not. The remainder of the writer's argument that Wu Han had been a strategist for Chiang is conducted on a similar level of banality, brings forth no evidence whatever in support of his contentions, and warrants no further space here.

Before leaving Li Ssu-chün's article, however, his handling of his second charge against Wu Han should also be noted. The accusation that he was a helper of American imperialism was, after all, the most serious charge ever brought against Wu Han. The evidence in support of it? Leighton Stuart, the American Ambassador to China, in his report of September 29, 1947, to Secretary of State Marshall, advocated American support of what he termed "the progressive elements" within and without the Chinese government in order that America could achieve her goals in China. In the 1950 American White Paper on China, Stuart is quoted as advocating a "third force" in China. As a member of the Democratic League, Wu Han belonged to a "third force." According to Li, this may be taken as concrete proof of an alliance between Wu Han and the Americans.

More relevant criticisms concerned with what Wu Han actually wrote on the subject of Hai Jui appeared in the CCP theoretical journal, *Red Flag*. Despite the abundance of rather banal political ranting appearing in the Chinese press as a whole at the time, *Red Flag* contained several articles of a relatively high analytical standard.[15] In view of the gravity of the charges made against Wu Han and his cohorts, it is necessary to examine all of them, despite the fact that many appear groundless. Because we have until now been systematically eliminating the weak or absurd charges hurled in the frenzy of the Cultural Revolution, the reader may have assumed that there is no case against the "Three-Family Village." This would be entirely incorrect. Although sometimes obscured by the type of polemic cited in the first part of this chapter, well-substantiated charges do appear both in Yao Wen-yuan's essays and in other analyses which appeared in the Chinese press.

Earlier we noted Mao Tse-tung's declaration that the class nature of any work of literature must be determined primarily on the basis of the class from which it draws its heroes.[16] The question of Hai Jui, a member of the feudal ruling class, being characterized by Wu Han as a saviour of the common people has already been discussed. It is noteworthy that Wu Han's glorification of the old scholar-official class was not an isolated phenomenon. Virtually everything written by Wu, Teng T'o, and Liao Mo-sha under the headings of "Evening Chats at Yen-shan" and "Notes from Three-Family Village" is centred around some aspect of pre-modern literature or aristocratic social life. *Jen Min Jih Pao* stated in an editorial of June 2, 1966,

On the cultural front, they have worked hard to let emperors and kings, generals and prime ministers, scholars and beauties, foreign idols and dead men dominate the stage.[17]

Yao Wen-yuan, once he frees himself from his obsession with historical details, makes some penetrating criticisms. Several of these were already raised at the beginning of this chapter without reference to Yao. They are simply noted here without discussion prior to consideration of a number of rational charges which have not been discussed as yet. Yao observes that in the play, once the land is returned to the peasants, "sharp class contradictions suddenly have no meaning whatsoever," even though the feudal system remains unchanged and the cruel exploitation and oppression by the landlords still exists. He argues that since, according to Marxist theory, the state is a machine through which one class oppresses another, all officials, including "honest ones" and "good ones," were of necessity members of the landlord class. But the play, says Yao, simply denies this. Wu Han is interpreted as saying that the honest official "is not a political instrument of the landlord class, but on the contrary is in the service of the peasantry." Wu has been charged by other critics as well with trying to portray the virtues of "good officials" as being above class.[18] Yao holds that in Wu Han's opinion the "good official," not the class struggle, constitutes the motive force of history.[19]

The masses of the people do not need to rise up and liberate themselves. They only need to wait for the kindness of an "honest official" or "your worship" and then they will immediately arrive upon "happy days."

105

He also raised the question of what Wu Han was asking readers to learn in the preface of the play. Are they to learn something about returning land, or perhaps about the "redress of injustices"?[20]

In the final analysis, the case against "Three-Family Village," *Hai Jui's Dismissal,* "Hai Jui Scolds the Emperor," and "On Hai Jui" must stand or fall on the basis of one accusation. Despite charges to the contrary, there is no conclusive evidence that any of the three writers attacked were acting in collusion with foreign powers. It is highly doubtful that Wu Han's manipulation of historical characters in itself constitutes any form of political satire. However, Yao Wen-yuan and others have also accused Wu Han of "using the past in order to satirize the present." Here they are on much more solid ground. When we ignore the accuracies or inaccuracies of the play in terms of Ming history and concentrate only on the political events transpiring in China at the time the play and the related essays appeared, it is not difficult to discern biting satire. Earlier, Yao Wen-yuan's contention that Wu Han built up his argument by "whitewashing" bad historical characters was held to be implausible on the ground that the audience's lack of detailed historical knowledge would render satire impossible. When the parallels are drawn between the stage play and current events, however, the requirements for parody are fulfilled. The remainder of this chapter is devoted to demonstrating that *Hai Jui's Dismissal* was in fact intended as an attack on Mao Tse-tung and as support for Marshal P'eng Teh-huai.

In the course of the long public discussion which followed the disclosure of the Wu-Teng-Liao alliance and the pervasive influence it enjoyed for a number of years through journals under its control, several comparisons were made with the Petofi Club in Hungary.[21] "Three-Family Village" and their followers have been regarded by elements loyal to Mao as the political arm of a similar counter-revolutionary movement. Their ridicule of party leaders and policies and their constant promotion of "bourgeois ideology" were seen as the necessary political groundwork for the restoration of capitalism.[22] Mao has taught the Chinese that before an established political order can be overthrown, the necessary ideological groundwork must be completed. According to Mao, "This is true for the revolutionary class as well as for the counter-revolutionary class."[23]

The chronology in the previous chapter began with the events surrounding the Lushan Conference of 1959. It was stated there that Defence Minister P'eng Teh-huai and a number of his supporters launched an attack on the party's Central Committee. This attack resulted in the dismissal of P'eng and his followers from their posts. The members of "Three-Family Village" were consistently accused of

106

co-ordinating their writings with the actions of the Right Opportunists, both before and after the Lushan Conference, and with systematically attacking the party over a period of years.[24] The evaluation of this charge depends largely on an examination of the dates of publication of important articles in relation to the occurrence of major political events.

The article "Hai Jui Scolds the Emperor" was published less than one month before P'eng Teh-huai sent his critical letter to Mao. The emphasis of the article is entirely on the courage of a minister in criticizing his superior. In the following month, P'eng Teh-huai was dismissed from his post as minister of defence. One month after P'eng's dismissal, on September 21, 1959, Wu Han published another article, "On Hai Jui." No longer emphasizing the matter of ministers criticizing their superiors, Wu's theme now became that of the "virtuous official" who has been unjustly dismissed from office. Perhaps it was mere coincidence that Wu Han's change of themes happened to coincide with the change in fortunes of the Right Opportunists. However, Wu Han became extremely interested in the question of "unjust dismissal" and over the next few years he culled other examples from Chinese history.[25] Perhaps it was simply a further coincidence, but between 1961 and 1963 Teng T'o also wrote four separate articles about "good officials" in Chinese history who had been dismissed from office. As one proceeds with an examination of the writings of "Three-Family Village," however, the number of occasions on which articles with possible double meanings coincide with major political events is seen greatly to exceed the laws of chance.

Yao Wen-yuan takes issue with Wu Han's statement of theme in the preface to *Hai Jui's Dismissal*. Although Wu claims that the final writing of the play took as its central theme the elimination of tyrannical landlords, Yao states that the main conflict of the drama occurs over the issue of "returning the land." According to Yao, the "high tide" is the dismissal of Hai Jui and this occurs because of the returning of the land. The land question in Wu Han's writing appears, in the views of most of his critics, to be an attack on the Great Leap Forward.[26] Yao also stresses Wu Han's emphasis and re-emphasis on the fact that "there are many injustices which must be reversed." In "On Hai Jui," Wu Han stated quite openly that modern people should oppose bureaucratism in the same way that bad officials were opposed in the olden days.

A *Red Flag* article in June 1966 specifically charged that the play *Hai Jui's Dismissal* was intended to sing the praises of the "Right Opportunist elements" who had been dismissed from office in 1959 and to encourage them not to submit, not to lose their spirit, and to

107

try again when they met failure.[27] The same article also accused Wu Han of encouraging these elements to "reassume political power and restore capitalism."

When he says in the preface that "he did not submit even though he lost his position, and did not lose his spirit ... that he deserves our study today," he has already made the central idea of *Hai Jui's Dismissal* absolutely clear.[28]

In the opinion of the authors of this article, Kuan Feng and Lin Chieh, two of the major purposes of the play are to stress the sympathy felt by the people for Hai Jui after his dismissal, and to use Hai Jui's statement that he will one day return to power as an opportunity to promise publicly that P'eng Teh-huai would also eventually triumph. It is in this article that the most weighty single argument is produced concerning Wu Han's real intentions in writing the play. The authors claim that at the time of the Lushan Conference, one of the Right Opportunists was actually referring to himself as "Hai Jui."[29] If this claim is valid, it surely constitutes quite concrete proof of Wu Han's intentions, when considered in conjunction with the chronological record. Unfortunately, Kuan and Lin do not elaborate.

Further evidence that Wu Han's writings were intended as political satires may be found by examining articles written by other members of "Three-Family Village" during the same period. At the Twenty-second Congress of the CPSU in October 1961, Nikita Khrushchov launched an open attack on Albania, and by extension, on the Chinese Communist Party as well.[30] Whether by coincidence or otherwise, this period saw a considerable upsurge in the publications by the Wu-Teng-Liao group. To cite but one example, in November Teng T'o published the article "Great Empty Talk."[31] In this essay, Teng wrote disparagingly of people who "talk ... like water flowing from an undammed river." "After listening to them," he says, "... you can remember nothing." He then tells us that his neighbour's little boy has developed the habit of indulging in meaningless clichés and "great empty talk." Recently he has written an absurd little poem:

The Venerable Heaven is our father,
The Great Earth is our mother
And the Sun is our nanny;
The East Wind is our benefactor
And the West Wind is our enemy.

There can be no doubt that this is a rather unsubtle attack on that theory of Mao Tse-tung's which Yao Wen-yuan calls the "scientific

Marxist-Leninist thesis that the East Wind prevails over the West Wind."[32] Teng T'o ends his article by advising

those friends given to great empty talk to read more, think more, say less and take a rest when the time comes for talking, so as to save their own as well as other people's time and energy.

Yao Wen-yuan strongly attacked Teng for articles which Yao interpreted as support for Soviet revisionism.[33] In one, Teng advocated that China unite with countries stronger than herself, and expressed satisfaction that China had stronger friends.[34] In a more pointed statement on the same theme, Teng T'o wrote,

If a man with a swelled head thinks he can learn a subject with ease and kicks his teacher out, he will never learn anything.[35]

The above quotation was seen by Yao Wen-yuan as a vicious attack on the Great Leap Forward and the policy of "self-reliance." In this period, Teng T'o wrote "The Family Wealth Consisting of a Single Egg," which was also widely interpreted as supporting Khrushchov's position on the Great Leap.[36] There are numerous other examples which can be cited, but the purpose of examining Teng T'o's writings is not to initiate a full discussion on them but to shed light on Wu Han's motives.

In case there should be any remaining doubt about the joint motivation of the members of "Three-Family Village," they themselves provide some of the most conclusive evidence. As mentioned in the previous chapter, the very name they selected was based on the story of the last days of a "virtuous official" who had been dismissed from office. Furthermore two of Teng T'o's articles consist of describing the methodology of satirists whom Teng admires.[37] One such description is particularly valuable for helping the reader to understand the real meanings of Liao Mo-sha's works. Liao's specialty within "Three-Family Village" was the writing of articles about ghosts. Lu Ting-i made a pointed reference to Liao in 1964 while stating that the ghost themes in a number of Peking operas supported revisionism.[38] Another critic who has achieved prominence in the course of the Cultural Revolution saw in the ghosts of Liao Mo-sha

the imperialists, revisionists, and reactionaries of various countries ... landlords, rich peasants, counter-revolutionaries, bad elements, and rightists.[39]

In writing of the career of an artist who drew satirical ghosts, Teng T'o states,

His satirical portrayal of ghosts is actually a satirical portrayal of men. ... If the artist had used the cartoon directly to satirize living men, he would simply have been asking for trouble. ... If he only satirized a few ghosts, he would be quite safe.[40]

To conclude their argument, Kuan Feng and Lin Chieh raised a number of valid points, mostly concerning the discrepancy between the content of Wu Han's early explanations of his interest in Hai Jui and the content of his later self-criticisms. They recalled that at the time "Hai Jui Scolds the Emperor" and "On Hai Jui" were written, Wu Han was urging his readers to study the past in order to apply its lessons to the present. In his self-criticism, however, Wu said that *Hai Jui's Dismissal* had no meaning whatever for the present and no political content. He said he had forgotten the principle that all art must serve the needs of the present-day political situation. In organizing their case against Wu, Kuan and Lin stressed that it was he who made the connection with the Lushan Conference.[41] Since Wu Han had claimed that he wrote "On Hai Jui" and *Hai Jui's Dismissal* only in response to the call by the Central Committee of the CCP at Lushan for a struggle against Right Opportunists,[42] Kuan and Lin insisted that the play be analysed in terms of its relationship to Lushan.

They pointed out that the claim of responding to the call of the Central Committee is simply tacked onto the end of Wu's essay and has no connection with what precedes it. It must also be noted that there is no explanation whatever of how the essay or the play fulfils the task of combatting Right Opportunists. Moreover, the argument that Right Opportunism could be exposed by taking a member of the ruling class and casting him in the role of saviour of the peasants is politically illogical and certainly requires explanation. The final blow is dealt Wu Han's claim of responding to the Central Committee's call when Kuan Feng and Lin Chieh draw attention to the fact that "Hai Jui Scolds the Emperor," the direct antecedent of "On Hai Jui" and *Hai Jui's Dismissal*, was published two months before the Lushan Conference took place. It is therefore clear that whatever Wu Han's plan at the time, he had "mounted horse" and was "in the saddle" before the Central Committee's call ever went out from Lushan.

NOTES AND BIBLIOGRAPHY

Notes

1 This occurred in January 1961, as noted in the chronology given in part two: The Charges.

2 A pavilion on the edge of the city where minor officials staged receptions for high officials coming to assume office.

3 A mountain northwest of Sungkiang County in Kiangsu province. See *Chung-Kuo Ku Chin Ti Ming Ta Tz'u-tien* (Taipei: Taiwan Commercial Press, 1967), p. 1219.

4 Ming Dynasty emperor, ruling from 1522 to 1567.

5 The Chinese character *Ao* which is used here is translated as "sea-turtle."

6 The Chinese for which the translation *Peking Gazette* is given is *Ti Pao*, meaning "newspaper of the capital," although this is not a literal translation. During the Han and T'ang dynasties, *Ti* was used to designate the lodgings for feudal princes in the capital. The term *Ti Pao* was applied to special mandates and orders of the court sent to the princes from their lodgings in the capital. Eventually the term came to be used for official newspapers of the capital. The term *Ti* came to mean an official residence.

7 The rhyme scheme of traditional T'ang Dynasty poetry.

8 An old Chinese saying, roughly the equivalent of "throw a sprat to catch a mackerel."

9 In order to provide a faithful translation of everything Wu Han wrote in his preface, this passage is translated even though the portrait, calligraphy, and historical notes are not reproduced here.

10 The "single whip policy" was a tax reform introduced during the last century of the Ming Dynasty. It was intended to overcome the gross corruption which had grown steadily under the *li-chia* system, which put responsibility for collecting government taxes in the hands of the wealthiest and most powerful families of each area. These powerful gentry families quite commonly forged land documents and registered their own land in the names of the poor. The latter then had to pay the taxes, though they were completely helpless to enforce any rights of ownership. Also, so many land, grain, and labour taxes were assessed against the common people that they were paying some sort of levy almost every month of the year. In many areas, the burden had be-

come so great that a large number of the people fled their land. The "single whip policy" combined this myriad of assessments into only one, or sometimes a few, payments. See Edwin O. Reischauer and John K. Fairbank, *East Asia: The Great Tradition* (Boston: Houghton Mifflin, 1960), pp. 337-40.

11 Literally "cultivated talents," this was the term used to denote a graduate of the first degree under the old examination system.

12 The meaning of *Ch'ing-ming* is literally "clear and bright." Here, it refers to a solar period beginning approximately April 5. At this time of the year, the Chinese traditionally visited their family graves.

13 CHAO is mistakenly rendered HUNG in the text but is corrected here.

14 The Chinese word *ku*, usually translated as orphan, is not the exact equivalent of the English term. It actually means "fatherless child."

15 This is a reference to a Sung Dynasty judge who established a reputation for redressing injustices.

16 The Chinese term here rendered as "scholar" is *sheng yuan*, meaning "a first-degree licentiate under the former system."

17 See note 11.

18 *Ch'ing-t'ien* is a polite term denoting an honest official.

19 The Gates of Heaven.

20 Wu District or County, referring to the Woosung-Shanghai area.

21 The translation of the characters *Po-p'i* is "to skin, to fleece, to extort, to rob the clothes off."

22 In ancient times, feudal lords of exceptionally great merit were honoured by being granted the privilege of using red gates. Hence doors painted red indicated high rank and the implication here is that the officials in this play were not entitled to the display of these red gates.

23 Meaning "resolute, firm, unyielding, lofty."

24 The date of Hai Jui's memorial was February 1566. See Wu Han, "Hai Jui Scolds the Emperor," in K. H. Fan, ed., *The Chinese Cultural Revolution: Selected Documents* (New York: Grove Press, 1968), pp. 72-6.

25 This is a pun based on the fact that the two characters designating the reign title of the emperor, *chia-ching*, have the same sound in Chinese as the two characters meaning "empty house."

26 An abbreviation referring to Suchow and Hangchow.

27 See note 21.

28 See note 10.

29 See note 10. The reference would appear to indicate that Hai Jui had done away with the practice of putting tax collection in the hands of a village headman, as had become the custom in the Ming Dynasty under the *li-chia* system.

30 This is the ancient name for Wu County in Kiangsu, dating from the Spring and Autumn period. See *Chung-Kuo Ku Chin Ti Ming Ta Tz'u-tien* (Taipei: Taiwan Commercial Press, 1967), p. 37.

31 A sword given by the emperor as a rare honour to officials who had distinguished themselves. The possessor was entitled to perform executions at his own discretion with this sword.

32 The literal meaning of Hsü Chieh's words is "beats to death." However, the reference is to the first beating of Chao Yu-shan, in which the latter was only injured.

33 Hai Lung Wang, according to Chinese mythology, is a dragon-king of the sea, with powers over the rivers, lakes, rains, and waters generally. He is said to have the power of providing prosperity and peace. See E. T. C. Werner, *A Dictionary of Chinese Mythology* (New York: Julian Press, 1961).

34 See note 15.

35 This phrase seems inapt in this context, yet the English expression is very close in meaning to the Chinese. Wu Han's method of expression seems awkward here.

36 In the reign of Emperor Shun Ti, during the Eastern Han Dynasty, the prime minister, Liang Yi, ordered a commission of eight men to go on a tour of inspection and examine the customs and morals of the empire. One of the eight, a censor named Chang Kang, had been campaigning against official corruption. He refused to go on the tour and as a symbol of his defiance he buried the wheels of his cart at the gates of the capital and uttered the statement, "While wolves are in office, why seek out foxes?" See Herbert A. Giles, *A Chinese Biographical Dictionary* (Taipei: Literature House).

37 The "Thousand Character Essay" was a standard exercise book for children learning to write characters. In this text, no single character is used more than once. The "Hundred Family Surnames," as the title implies, was a compilation of Chinese surnames, and this also formed a standard text for students beginning their study of the Chinese written language. Hsü Fu at this point completely exposes himself because these two well-known texts could not possibly be mistaken for original essays, and also because no educated Chinese would spend his time writing them out.

38 Here Hsü Fu is referring to the black silk cap which could be worn only by a *hsiu-ts'ai*.

39 A polite term used by Hai Jui in this case as a form of address to the peasants whom he had befriended.

40 Wu Han tells us that this scene occurs three days after the trial has taken place. The phrase "day before yesterday" therefore seems to be inaccurate, but this is what appears in the Chinese text.

41 A Chinese measure of land which is approximately equal to one-sixth of an acre.

42 A supervising censor.

THE CHARGES

1 "Never Forget the Class Struggle," *Liberation Army Daily* (Shanghai), May 4, 1966, reprinted in *The Great Socialist Cultural Revolution in China (1)* (Peking: Foreign Languages Press, 1966), pp. 20-8; "China in the Midst of High-Tide of the Great Proletarian Cultural Revolution," *Chinese Literature,* no. 8, 1966, reprinted in Asia Research Centre, ed., *The Great Cultural Revolution in China* (Rutland and Tokyo: Charles E. Tuttle, 1968), pp. 304-12; "Long Live the Great Proletarian Cultural Revolution," *Red Flag,* no. 8, 1966, reprinted in *The Great Socialist Cultural Revolution in China (4)* (Peking: Foreign Languages Press, 1966), pp. 1-19.

2 Mao Tse-tung, "Talks at the Yenan Forum on Literature and Art," *Selected Works of Mao Tse-tung* (Peking: Foreign Languages Press, 1965), vol. III, p. 86.

3 "Never Forget the Class Struggle," p. 23; Kao Chu, "Open Fire at the Black Anti-Party and Anti-Socialist Line," *Liberation Army Daily,* May 8, 1966, reprinted in *The Great Socialist Cultural Revolution in China (2)* (Peking: Foreign Languages Press, 1966). "Mao Tse-tung's Thought is the Telescope and Microscope of Our Revolutionary Cause," (Liberation Army Daily, June 7, 1966), reprinted in *The Great Socialist Cultural Revolution in China (3)*, pp. 11-17. It may strike English readers that this sentiment is strikingly reminiscent of the popular Western adage that the pen is mightier than the sword. It is interesting to note that in ancient China there was an almost parallel popular saying which may be translated as, "Other people have their swords, but I have a brush as sharp as a knife."

4 See Richard H. Solomon, "One Party and 'One Hundred Schools'; Leadership, Lethargy, or *Luan*," *Current Scene,* vol. VII, nos. 19-20 (October 1, 1969).

5 "New Victory for Mao Tse-tung's Thought," *Jen Min Jih Pao,* June 4, 1966.

6 K. H. Fan, ed., *The Chinese Cultural Revolution: Selected Documents* (New York: Grove Press, 1968), p. 65.

7 "Resolution of Eighth Plenary Session of Eighth Central Committee of CCP Concerning the Anti-Party Clique Headed by P'eng Teh-huai," in Fan, *ibid.,* p. 67.

8 *Ibid.*

9 David Floyd, *Mao against Khrushchov: A Short History of the Sino-Soviet Conflict* (New York and London: Praeger, 1963), p. 66.

116

10 David A. Charles, "The Dismissal of Marshal P'eng Teh-huai," *China Quarterly,* no. 8 (October-December 1961), p. 64.

11 Floyd, *Mao against Khrushchov,* p. 67.

12 *Ibid.*

13 "Resolution of Eighth Plenary Session of Eighth Central Committee of CCP Concerning the Anti-Party Clique Headed by P'eng Teh-huai," in Fan, *The Chinese Cultural Revolution,* pp. 66-72.

14 Editor's Note, *Ming Pao* (April, 1966), p. 67.

15 Yao Wen-yuan, "On 'Three-Family Village': The Reactionary Nature of *Evening Chats at Yenshan* and *Notes from Three-Family Village,*" in *Liberation Daily* (May 10, 1966), reprinted in *The Great Socialist Cultural Revolution in China (1)* (Peking: Foreign Languages Press, 1966), p. 46.

16 Teng T'o is a former editor of *Jen Min Jih Pao.* He was Secretary of the Peking Municipal Party Committee prior to June 1966, when that body was reorganized. Until the month before, he had also been editor-in-chief of the *Peking Daily, Peking Evening News,* and the fortnightly magazine, *Frontline.* In 1964 he was elected deputy for Peking to the Third National People's Congress, and in 1965 he became an alternate member of the CCP North China Bureau.

17 See quotations from his essay, "Great Empty Talk," in the following chapter.

18 Yao Wen-yuan, "On 'Three-Family Village,'" p. 43.

19 *Ibid.*

20 *Ibid.*

21 Fan, *The Chinese Cultural Revolution,* p. 65. Liao Mo-sha is the former director of the United Front Work Department of the Peking Municipal Committee of the CCP.

22 Beginning in late April 1966, dozens of articles attacking "Three-Family Village" appeared in the pages of *Jen Min Jih Pao* and *Red Flag.* The writer can state on the basis of personal experience in China in October 1966 that even at this time it seemed impossible to engage a Chinese citizen in a discussion of the Cultural Revolution which did not centre on the threat which "Three-Family Village" posed to the party.

23 *Liberation Daily* (Shanghai, May 21, 1966). Cited in Asia Research Centre, ed., *The Great Cultural Revolution,* pp. 177-8.

24 Lin Chieh *et al.,* "Teng T'o's *Evening Chats at Yenshan* is Anti-Party and Anti-Socialist Double-Talk," *Liberation Army Daily* (May 8, 1966), reprinted in *The Great Socialist Cultural Revolution in China (2)* (Peking: Foreign Languages Press, (1966), p. 38.

25 Yao Wen-yuan, "On 'Three-Family Village,'" p. 47.

26 *Ibid.*

27 *Ibid.*

28 *Ibid.*, p. 53.

29 *Ibid.*

30 *Ibid.*

31 *Ibid.*, p. 62.

32 *Ibid.*

33 *Ibid.*

34 *Ibid.*, p. 64.

35 *Ibid.*

36 Lu Ting-i, Speech at the opening of the 1964 Festival of Peking Opera on Contemporary Themes, June 5, 1964. Asian Research Centre, ed., *The Great Cultural Revolution*, p. 29.

37 *Ibid.*

38 "Raise High the Great Red Banner of Mao Tse-tung's Thought and Carry the Great Proletarian Cultural Revolution Through to the End: *Essential Points for Propaganda and Education in Connection with the Great Cultural Revolution,*" *Liberation Army Daily,* June 6, 1966. Reprinted in *The Great Socialist Cultural Revolution in China (5)* (Peking: Foreign Languages Press, 1966), pp. 8-9.

39 "Long Live the Great Proletarian Cultural Revolution," *Red Flag,* no. 8, 1966, reprinted in *The Great Socialist Cultural Revolution in China (4),* pp. 1-19; "Raise High the Great Red Banner," p. 6.

40 "China in the Midst of High-Tide of the Great Proletarian Cultural Revolution," p. 306.

41 See note 39.

42 Ting Kuang-hua, "The Climax in the Struggle of 'Cultural Revolution,'" *Chinese Communist Affairs,* vol. 3, no. 4 (August 1966), p. 36.

43 Asia Research Centre, ed., *The Great Cultural Revolution,* p. 419.

44 *Ibid.*

45 *Ibid.*, p. 91.

46 "Commemorate Lu Hsun and Carry the Revolution Through to the End," speech by Yao Wen-yuan, *Peking Review,* no. 45 (November 4, 1966), p. 12.

47 Yao's photograph has appeared in *Peking Review* on October 27, and December 25, 1967, and February 2 and June 28, 1968.

48 Chi Pen-yu, "On the Bourgeois Stand of *Frontline* and the *Peking Daily,*" *Red Flag,* no. 7 (1966). Reprinted in *The Great Socialist Cultural Revolution in China (2),* pp. 50-65.

49 *Ibid.*, p. 51.

50 *Ibid.*

51 Yao Wen-yuan, "On 'Three-Family Village,'"

52 The fact that *Jen Min Jih Pao* published a self-criticism which was later held to be a sham may be significant, as Lu Ting-i's later fall

from power was linked to the lack of enthusiasm exhibited by *Jen Min Jih Pao* in the initial stages of the Cultural Revolution.

53 See Asia Research Centre, ed., *The Great Cultural Revolution*, pp. 194-204.

54 T'ien Han was chairman of the Union of Chinese Drama Workers, vice-chairman of the All-China Federation of Literary and Art Circles, and the writer of China's national anthem. He was subjected to fierce attack in *Jen Min Jih Pao* and other Chinese newspapers throughout 1966, and eventually was accused of working for Chiang K'ai-shek.

55 Yao Wen-yuan, "On 'Three-Family Village,'" p. 64.

56 Chi Pen-yu, "On the Bourgeois Stand," p. 54.

57 Wan Ta-hung, "The Suicidal Purge Campaign," *Chinese Communist Affairs*, vol. 3, no. 4 (August 1966), p. 26.

58 Asia Research Centre, ed., *The Great Cultural Revolution*, p. 169.

59 "Expose Wu Han's True Social Standing," *Jen Min Jih Pao*, May 20, 1966.

60 "Wu Han and Hu Shih," *Jen Min Jih Pao*, April 13, 1966.

61 *Ibid.*

62 For an English summary of the main charges in this article, see Asia Research Centre, ed., *The Great Cultural Revolution*, p. 187.

63 Yao Wen-yuan, "On 'Three-Family Village,'" p. 29.

64 *Ibid.*, pp. 30-1.

65 Kau Chu, "Open Fire"; Lin Chieh *et al.*, "Double-Talk." The article by Lin Chieh's group is particularly valuable because it reproduces a great number of the articles carried under the titles of "Evening Chats at Yenshan" and "Three-Family Village." There is a short analysis and commentary after each article.

66 Chi Pen-yu, "On the Bourgeois Stand."

67 Lin Chieh, "Expose Teng T'o's Anti-Party and Anti-Socialist Features."

68 Asia Research Centre, ed., *The Great Cultural Revolution*, p. 494.

69 *Ibid.*, p. 495.

70 *Ibid.*

71 *Ibid.*

72 *Ibid.* In the June 5 edition of *Jen Min Jih Pao*, Lu was accused of allowing Peking University to be used by members of the former Peking Municipal Committee as an instrument for gaining the allegiance of students, attempting to spread "revisionism" and discriminating against students of worker and peasant backgrounds.

73 As noted earlier, since May 25 *Jen Min Jih Pao* had been raising the question of who had been responsible for allowing "Three-Family Village" to function for such a long period.

119

74 Chi Pen-yu, "On the Bourgeois Stand," p. 50.
75 Asia Research Centre, ed., *The Great Cultural Revolution*, p. 497.
76 *Ibid.*, p. 167.
77 *Ibid.*, p. 168.
78 Asia Research Centre, ed., *The Great Cultural Revolution.*

EVALUATION OF THE CHARGES

1 See Yao Wen-yuan, "On 'Three-Family Village': The Reactionary Nature of *Evening Chats at Yenshan* and *Notes from Three-Family Village,*" in *Liberation Daily* (May 10, 1966), reprinted in *The Great Socialist Cultural Revolution in China (1)* (Peking: Foreign Languages Press, 1966).
2 *Jen Min Jih Pao* (September 21, 1959).
3 *Ibid.*
4 Stephen Uhalley, Jr. "The Cultural Revolution and the Attack on the 'Three-Family Village,'" *China Quarterly*, no. 27 (July-September 1966), p. 150.
5 *Who's Who in Communist China* (Hong Kong: Union Research Institute, 1966), p. 636.
6 *Jen Min Jih Pao* (December 30, 1965, and January 12, 1966).
7 E.g.: "slandering the party line for socialist construction as 'forced' and claiming that China's 'only out' is to learn from the Soviet revisionist clique and practise revisionism in China." Yao Wen-yuan, "On 'Three-Family Village,'" p. 42.
8 *Ibid.*, p. 40.
9 "Everybody knows that the great Chinese Communist Party and the great Chinese people, educated by Mao Tse-tung's thought, are not only not afraid of monsters and ghosts, but are determined to destroy all the monsters and ghosts in the world." *Ibid.*, p. 49.
10 A rather complicated procedure, involving the registration of one man's land in the name of another, in order to circumvent the highest tax rates, is discussed in some detail by Yao in this article.
11 Identified by Yao as the biggest landlord in the area under Hai Jui's jurisdiction.
12 See Kuan Feng and Lin Chieh, "'Hai Jui Scolds the Emperor' and *Hai Jui's Dismissal* are Two Great Anti-Party, Anti-Socialist Poisonous Weeds," *Red Flag*, no. 5 (1966), pp. 15-33.
13 Yao Wen-yuan, "On the New Historical Drama *Hai Jui's Dismissal,*" *Wen Hui Pao* (Shanghai, November 10, 1965).
14 This is a theme which pervades almost all the military writings of Mao Tse-tung.
15 Kuan Feng and Lin Chieh, "Poisonous Weeds"; Chi Pen-yu, "On the Bourgeois Stand of *Frontline* and the *Peking Daily,*" *Red Flag*, no. 7

120

(1966); "Long Live the Great Proletarian Cultural Revolution," editorial, *Red Flag*, no. 8 (1966).

16 Mao Tse-tung, "Talks at the Yenan Forum on Literature and Art," *Selected Works of Mao Tse-tung*, vol. III (Peking: Foreign Languages Press, 1966), pp. 7-10.

17 "A Great Revolution That Touches People to Their Very Souls," *The Great Socialist Cultural Revolution in China* (Peking: Foreign Languages Press, 1966), pp. 7-10.

18 *Jen Min Jih Pao* (May 8, 1966).

19 Mao Tse-tung has stated, "The people and the people alone are the motive force of world history." *Selected Works of Mao Tse-tung*, vol. III (Peking: Foreign Languages Press, 1965), p. 257.

20 See p. 88 for Yao's elaboration of this question.

21 "Long Live the Great Proletarian Cultural Revolution," *Red Flag*, no. 8 (1966), reprinted in *The Great Socialist Cultural Revolution in China (3)*, pp. 1-19.

22 In one of his "Evening Chats at Yenshan," Teng T'o discussed the old practice of writing up the biographies of the important gentry in each locality; he seems to suggest that the famous gentry of the Peking area should be written up in this fashion. Yao charges that this is an "attempt at restoration in the most profound sense of the term." He also accuses the members of the "Three-Family Village" of going so far as to advocate the return of the old Confucian style of greeting (the clasping of the hands in front of the body), and of indulging themselves in gluttony and the pursuit of bourgeois pleasures. Unfortunately, he gives no references to substantiate these charges. See Yao Wen-yuan, "On 'Three-Family Village,'" pp. 59-61.

23 *Decision of the Central Committee of the Chinese Communist Party Concerning the Great Proletarian Cultural Revolution* (Peking: Foreign Languages Press, 1966), p. 1.

24 "Raise High the Great Red Banner of Chairman Mao's Thought and Carry the Great Proletarian Cultural Revolution Through to the End," *Liberation Army Daily* (June 6, 1966), reprinted in *The Great Socialist Cultural Revolution in China (5)* (Peking: Foreign Languages Press, 1966).

25 Yao Wen-yuan, "On 'Three-Family Village,'" p. 43.

26 Wu's consistent emphasis of this theme has been taken as opposition to the collectivization of land formerly owned privately by peasants.

27 Kuan Feng and Lin Chieh, "Poisonous Weeds."

28 *Ibid.*

29 *Ibid.*

30 David Floyd, *Mao Against Khrushchov: A Short History of the Sino-Soviet Conflict* (New York and London: Praeger, 1963), p. 145.

31 In "Evening Chats at Yenshan," *Peking Daily* (November 10, 1961). See Yao Wen-yuan, "On 'Three-Family Village,'" p. 48.

32 Yao Wen-yuan, *ibid.*

33 *Ibid.*, p. 42.

34 *Ibid.*

35 *Ibid.*

36 Lin Chieh *et al.*, "Teng T'o's *Evening Chats at Yenshan* is Anti-Party and Anti-Socialist Double-Talk," *Liberation Army Daily* (May 8, 1966), reprinted in *The Great Socialist Cultural Revolution in China (2)* (Peking: Foreign Languages Press, 1966).

37 *Ibid.*, pp. 41-2, 45-6.

38 Lu Ting-i, speech at the opening of the 1964 Festival of Peking Opera on Contemporary Themes, June 5, 1964. See Asia Research Centre, ed., *The Great Cultural Revolution in China* (Rutland and Tokyo: Charles E. Tuttle, 1968), p. 29.

39 Chi Pen-yu, "On the Bourgeois Stand of *Frontline* and the *Peking Daily*," *Red Flag*, no. 7 (1966), reprinted in *The Great Socialist Cultural Revolution in China (2)*, pp. 50-65.

40 Lin Chieh *et al.*, "Double Talk," pp. 45-6.

41 Kuan Feng and Lin Chieh, "Poisonous Weeds."

42 Wu Han, "On Hai Jui," *Jen Min Jih Pao* (September 21, 1959).

Bibliography

SOURCES IN ENGLISH

Asia Research Centre, ed. *The Great Cultural Revolution in China.* Rutland and Tokyo: Charles E. Tuttle, 1968.

Charles, David A. "The Dismissal of Marshal P'eng Teh-huai." *China Quarterly,* no. 8 (October-December 1961), pp. 63-76.

Fan, K. H., ed. *The Chinese Cultural Revolution: Selected Documents.* New York: Grove Press, 1968.

Feng Wen. "Assumptions and Proofs of Mao-Liu Power Struggle." *Chinese Communist Affairs,* vol. 3, no. 4 (August 1966), pp. 47-55.

Floyd, David. *Mao against Khrushchov: A Short History of the Sino-Soviet Conflict.* New York and London: Praeger, 1963.

Giles, Herbert A. *A Chinese Biographical Dictionary.* Reprint, Taipei: Literature House.

Goldman, Merle. "The Fall of Chou Yang." *China Quarterly,* no. 27 (July-September 1966), pp. 132-48.

The Great Socialist Cultural Revolution in China. Series of 7 pamphlets. Peking: Foreign Languages Press, 1966.

Griffith, William E. *The Sino-Soviet Rift.* Cambridge, Mass.: M.I.T. Press, 1964.

Joffe, Ellis. "China in Mid-1966. 'Cultural Revolution' or Struggle for Power?" *China Quarterly,* no. 27 (July-September 1966), pp. 123-31.

Mao Tse-tung. "Talks at the Yenan Forum on Literature and Art." *Selected Works of Mao Tse-tung,* vol. III. Peking: Foreign Languages Press, 1965.

Reischauer, Edwin O. and John K. Fairbank. *East Asia: The Great Tradition.* Boston: Houghton Mifflin Company, 1960.

Solomon, Richard H. "One Party and 'One Hundred Schools': Leadership, Lethargy, or Luan?" *Current Scene,* vol. VII, no. 19-20 (October 1, 1969).

Ting Kuang-hua. "The Climax in the Struggle of 'Cultural Revolution.'" *Chinese Communist Affairs,* vol. III, no. 4 (August 1966), pp. 33-41.

Ting Wang. "Yao Wen-yuan: Newcomer in China's Politburo." *Current Scene,* vol. VII, no. 14 (July 15, 1969).

Uhalley, Stephen Jr. "The Cultural Revolution and the Attack on the 'Three-Family Village.'" *China Quarterly,* no. 27 (July-September 1966), pp. 149-61.

123

Wan Ta-hung. "The Suicidal Purge Campaign." *Chinese Communist Affairs,* vol. III, no. 4 (August 1966), pp. 23-32.

Wu Chi-yen. "Repudiate Chou Yang's Revisionist Programme for Literature and Art." *Chinese Literature,* no. 10 (1966), pp. 112-40.

Zagoria, Donald S. *The Sino-Soviet Conflict, 1956-1961.* New York: Princeton University Press, 1964.

SOURCES IN CHINESE

吳晗，「論海瑞」，人民日報 (1959.9.21)，明報月刊 (香港)，1966年四月。

姚文元，「評新編歷史劇"海瑞罷官"」(1965.11.10載於文匯報)，收穫，6,1965。

關鋒　林杰「"海瑞罵皇帝"和"海瑞罷官"是反黨反社會主義的兩株大毒草」，紅旗，5,1966。

馬岩，「評吳晗同志的資產階級歷史觀」，紅旗，2,1966。

史紹賓「評吳晗的"報槍集"」；「工農兵羣眾批判吳晗反黨反社會主義的政治立場和學術觀點」，紅旗，6,1966。

「工農兵向反黨反社會主義分子開火」，紅旗，7,1966。

史紹賓，「胡适與吳晗」，人民日報，1966.4.13。

黎斯翠，「吳晗—— 蔣家王朝的策士，美帝的幫辦」，人民日報，1966.4.27。

丁偉志　王正萍，「剝開吳晗"民主斗士"的畫皮」，人民日報，1966.5.3。

「工農兵批判吳晗反黨反社會主義的立場和思想」，人民日報，1966.5.4。

譚文興，「評吳晗宣揚的"敢"的精神」；文朝暉，「駁吳晗的"用人唯才論"」；寇世瑛　金麗華，「美帝國主義精神侵略的辯護士」，人民日報，1966.5.5。

周英　凡英，「評李瑛的"評吳晗同志的歷史觀"」，人民日報，1966.5.5。

李希凡，「在吳晗的"學術"活動中貫串着一條甚麼黑線？」；「工農兵批判吳晗反黨反社會主義的立場和思想」，人民日報，1962.5.6。

徐遜，「吳晗的"清官"論是徹底徹尾的修正主義貨色，人民日報，1966.5.8。

林杰等，「鄧拓的"燕山夜話"是反黨反社會主義的黑話，人民日報，1966.5.9。

林杰，「揭破鄧拓反黨反社會主義的面目」，人民日報，1966.5.14。

齊力並進，「揭露吳晗的反革命眞面目」，人民日報，1966.
5.20

鮑文蔚等，「請看"三家村"的反動眞面目」，人民日報，
1966.5.15。

鄭公盈，「"北京文藝"在爲誰服務？」，人民日報，1966.
5.20。

「積極參加社會主義文化大革命，徹底搞掉反黨反社會主義
黑線」，人民日報，1966.5.24。

方澤生，「"海瑞上疏"必須繼續批判」；丁學雷，「"海瑞
上疏"爲誰效勞？」，人民日報，1966.5.28。

鄧拓。燕山夜話。（自聯出版社印行：香港，1966年）

臧勵龢等編。中國古今地名大辭典。（商務印書館：台灣，
民國五十五年）